'When I was a young Chri
to hear many sermons abo
One of the weaknesses of
our attempts to engage w
have perhaps played down ...., the biblical
focus on the second coming as well as on the hope of
heaven. That weakness needs to be addressed, and Pete
Lowman has done us a great service in attempting to bring
to the fore once again the biblical teaching on the certainty
of Christ's coming. Even if some readers may hold a
different perspective on the detail, we should all heed the
urgent call to watch and pray and to live in the light of the
certainty of Christ's return, His judgement on the
unbelieving world and the hope of heaven – a great
comfort to God's people.'
Lindsay Brown, former international director of IFES

'Pete Lowman has written this racy little book because he
wants us to be joyously enthusiastic and confident about
the second coming of Jesus, the end of history and the
defeat of evil. Carefully exploring and laying out the
premillennial view (a phrase he dislikes), Pete shows how
our understanding of the last days should be a powerful
motivation for radical holiness and evangelism. Not
everyone will agree with Pete's reading (I don't!). But,
nevertheless, this book will excite anyone about God's plan
for the future and encourage you get to grips with what the
Bible says about the greatest thing still to happen to Planet
Earth!'
Marcus Honeysett, director of Living Leadership

A Guide to the End of the World

Pete Lowman

instant
apostle

First published in Great Britain in 2018

Instant Apostle
The Barn
1 Watford House Lane
Watford
Herts
WD17 1BJ

British Library Cataloguing-in-Publication Data

A catalogue record for this book is available from the British
Library

This book and all other Instant Apostle books are available from
Instant Apostle:

Website: www.instantapostle.com

E-mail: info@instantapostle.com

ISBN 978-1-909728-85-1

Printed in Great Britain

Contents

Introduction

What You Will Get Out of This Book

Jesus comes back. History ends. A whole new world comes.
Huge things, vital things, thrilling things.
Which lots of us feel we don't have a clue about.
This book is meant to help remedy that!

We've many of us been in the situation – at home group perhaps – where Jesus' return comes up in conversation; and then perhaps the 'rapture', or the 'antichrist', or the 'millennium'. And suddenly there's an awkward silence in the room, and we find ourselves thinking... Do I believe in this? I'm not sure! (Does our pastor? Maybe they're not sure either!) And after all that, heaven – but what's that like?

It's easy to see why we're uncertain. What the Bible has to say about the future can be complex and difficult to grasp; and people have varying views about it. So, many of us simply don't engage with it. Worse, sometimes we hear that it's (again) become a space for unhelpful, even disastrous speculation: with Christians getting into the news through making ludicrous claims about when the world will end, or who among our current politicians is secretly the end-time satanic dictator. Googling 'Trump antichrist' turns up a range of websites revealing this as the Donald's true evil identity (after all, his family does own 666 Fifth Avenue, and in the first year of his presidency the US budget deficit apparently rose to 666 billion dollars!). But then, googling 'Obama antichrist' shows that Trump is not the only contender; indeed, a 2013 poll showed that 13 per cent of Americans thought Obama might be the evil being Revelation was talking about.[1] (Why does our UK prime minister not even get a look in?) And yes, we know this daft stuff happens because the people concerned just haven't got a grip on what the Bible says about it all – but, have we?

And then one of our friends says they saw the *Left Behind* film on Channel 5, or the hugely acclaimed *Leftovers* series on Sky Atlantic, or the horror film *The Remaining* directed by Casey La Scala of *Donnie Darko* fame. And all three have been about the aftermath of the 'rapture' (or the 'Sudden Departure'), an event when millions of people vanished from the earth, suddenly, and completely unexpectedly. And – what do we think about that?

After all, the idea of the 'rapture' wasn't invented by the creators of these shows. Large numbers of Christians worldwide think this is indeed how our Bible says history will close and how the end times, humanity's final, horrendous crisis, will come upon those tragically 'left behind'. In Britain, however, the idea is far less familiar. Some of us may have vaguely heard of it in negative comments by Richard Dawkins, or Brian McLaren, or maybe Tom Wright. But (in my experience at least) many British Christians have little idea whether, biblically, we should believe in the 'rapture' or not (or the 'antichrist', or the 'millennium'); and if not, just what, biblically, we should expect the future to hold.

So here's why it matters...

Perhaps these uncertainties about the 'rapture', 'antichrist' and 'millennium' aren't crucial (though if what I've just described does feel familiar, this book will give you tools to change the situation). But something else does matter – a lot.

The fact that one day the world as we know it will end, that Christ our Lord and Friend and Master will visibly return, is one of the most important and joyous Christian doctrines. A huge amount of Jesus' teaching, and of the New Testament as a whole, is dedicated to it (every twentieth verse in the New Testament, it's been calculated, and parts of every New Testament book except the three tiny books of Philemon, 2 John and 3 John). These were themes the old communist dictatorships were very keen to ensure that churches shouldn't preach, because they knew just how explosive they could be in people's lives.

But – in my experience – they're not taught much in British churches, and they're understood even less. So there are whole chunks of the Bible we approach unhappily, knowing we don't have much idea what they're talking about; and by and large we give up on them; to our deep impoverishment.

And yes, it is striking how different the situation has been on the other side of the Atlantic. Some years ago an American author called Tim LaHaye, who till then was mainly known for an explicit (but Bible-based and actually very helpful) book on sex called *The Act of Marriage*, produced a whole series of bestselling novels about the end of history and Christ's return, called *Left Behind*. The characters were a bit wooden, but in America the sales were huge (more than 60 million); they were stacked high in American airport bookshops. *The Simpsons* dedicated an episode to parodying the series. Here in Britain, however, they were almost unknown. And when the surprisingly powerful 2014 *Left Behind* film, starring Nicholas Cage, was released worldwide in commercial cinemas, we didn't see it in Britain at all. (Intriguingly, it was a huge hit in Lebanon, the Philippines and even the United Arab Emirates.) The whole subject doesn't seem to interest us.

I wonder if there are sociological reasons for this. Is there something in the English nature (as distinct from the Celtic, French or Russian natures), and especially perhaps in our Anglican state Church nature, that really doesn't like anything too drastic or apocalyptic, and hankers after the hope that all things will ultimately continue within the bounds of moderation?

Here's what pushed me to write this book. Broadly speaking, there are two kinds of approaches to the many prophetic, end-of-the-world, second-coming chunks of the Bible. First, there are what I'm going to call the more 'literal' approaches – meaning, they tend to take more literally what the Bible says about a huge final crisis-period of history lasting forty-two months, and a demonically inspired dictator ('the Animal') at the heart of it, and (for some) a dramatic intervention where God rescues His people (that's the 'rapture'); and then, after Christ returns in power, a 1,000-year period (the 'millennium') where He turns this earth back into paradise.

And then there are what I'm going to call the 'non-literal' approaches. That doesn't mean at all that their proponents deny that the Bible is totally inspired and reliable; I'm very aware that the 'non-literalist' brothers and sisters I fellowship with would insist they do take Scripture literally as and when that's appropriate. But this approach does tend to be characterised by some or all of our not being literally caught up into the air with Christ, there not being a literal three-and-a-half-year final crisis, there not being a literal end-time ultimate dictator, there not being a literal 1,000-year reign of Christ where Satan literally deceives the nations no more, and the wolf literally lies down with the lamb, etc. And so that final crisis, and the 'Animal' (the 'beast'), and the 'rapture', and the 'millennium', tend to be interpreted in ways other than what we might expect at face value: these things are speaking symbolically, or perhaps colourfully, to illustrate things that have been happening ever since the crucifixion, and so forth.

These more 'non-literal' approaches are overwhelmingly our dominant orthodoxy here in Britain. Not worldwide: an interesting survey[2] showed that worldwide the majority of evangelical Christian leaders believe in the 'rapture'. But lots of British churches, and many of our Bible colleges, wouldn't touch that kind of thing with a bargepole. The consequences, however, have been unfortunate. And it's not just that, when disbelieving in 'the rapture and all that', most of us British Christians have little idea as to why we so disbelieve. Something is happening that's much more unfortunate than this.

Let me nail my own colours to the mast here. It seems to me that the more 'non-literal' approaches often need a way of interpreting these Bible sections (a 'hermeneutic', to use the technical term) that involves saying, 'This doesn't mean what it first appears to mean.' (For example, about the 'millennium' or about the end-time dictator.) But as a result, large chunks of Scripture like Revelation, or the last quarter of Ezekiel, or of Daniel, or of Zechariah, come to seem difficult, potentially deceptive; anyway, intimidating. And therefore they can get neglected. (It seems to me that a strong argument for the more literal approach [or 'hermeneutic'] is that its proponents obviously find these books make straightforward sense and get excited and inspired by them and love delving into them, whereas the non-literal commentators can make them sound very daunting and confusing: the back covers of their works are often full of ominous comments about 'abstruse symbolism', 'bizarre imagery' and the like. In science, the best theory is one that makes uncomplicated sense of the maximum amount of data; apply that here and the 'literalists' win hands down.)

But here's what's really unfortunate for us. These 'literal' approaches to the final crisis, the final dictator and so on are almost unknown in Britain; it's extremely hard to find a good book setting them out that isn't culturally very much from across the Atlantic. That's what first motivated me to write what follows: to set out briefly the more 'literal'

14

understanding of these crucial matters, so that my readers know what the relevant Bible passages are, and can reflect on them and decide for themselves. (Either get excited about these vividly colourful and far-reaching ideas, or at least know what they are and why you see it differently!) But what's troubled me more has been realising how far this entire area of Jesus' second coming, from *any* perspective, has gone off the radar – to our vast impoverishment. (It's a pity too that in these same years the media have been talking about history as we know it ending – through global warming, etc – right when Britain's Bible Christians have stopped.)

As I prepared to write, I asked three well-informed Christian leaders, people who read widely and also move widely in their ministries, what currently were the key books on these areas. I expected these would all be from the 'non-literal' side, that being our British orthodoxy. To my surprise all three said the same thing: they were not aware of any really significant British title at present.[3] In other words, not only do most of us British Christians have almost no idea of the thrills and spills of the unorthodox, 'literal' view of the end times; our British, 'non-literal' doctrines about these things have lost the power to interest us as well. (I suspect because if people keep on telling us that certain topics or Bible books are confusing and puzzling, sooner or later we will just leave well alone.)

So here's what you should have when you finish this book: a grasp of at least one coherent way of thinking about these incredibly important matters. You'll know where to read about them in the Bible, and will be able to decide for yourself about them. (Incidentally, I myself am not totally convinced about some of what I'll be setting out, but I do think these are ways of putting together what the Bible says that deserve consideration, hence should at least be *known*.) We're going to look at a large number of Bible passages, not just to bolster any particular argument, but also to help us grow familiar with the huge wealth of Scriptures on this topic, and draw strength and encouragement from them, irrespective of the conclusions we end up with. (That's going to be particularly true when we turn to the joyous glory of what the Bible says about heaven!)

What matters above all is that we come to engage more with Jesus our coming King, to worship Him more, to long more for His return and for our life with Him in heaven, as the result of our venturing into these neglected passages. May it be so as we feed on His Word in the company of His Spirit!

Lastly, what this book doesn't do

One thing that has helped render this whole area impenetrable is the long words usually involved, and the hackneyed jokes made about them: premillennialism, amillennialism, and so forth. Therefore this book doesn't use those two words, except in this paragraph right here, and a few times more towards the end. By the more 'literal' approach I mean what is usually and mouth-fillingly called 'premillennialism', and by the 'non-literal' approach I mean what is usually called 'amillennialism'. To fans of seven-syllable words I can only offer my apologies.[4]

And there are other, less popular approaches – 'postmillennialism', 'preterism' – that won't get much coverage here, because this book's aim is just to set out the more 'literal' view of the end of the world for exploration.

This brings us on to another thing this book isn't: it isn't a scholarly defence of this approach. One of the main current American defences of the alternative, 'non-literal' approach is 550 pages long, and anyone wanting to joust seriously with that brother should write at similar depth and length. Such a scholarly account (and written on this side of the Atlantic) needs to exist, but this is not it. As a result there are many aspects it doesn't have space for. It aims simply to help bring Jesus' second coming, and what God says about the End, and joyous enthusiasm about these, back into our conversational space; and to help us look confidently and enthusiastically at the chunks of the Bible that present these things, and work them through for ourselves.

And most important: so that we can get back to a lifestyle in which – maybe in hope of the 'rapture', or maybe not – it is a live, joyous, life-transforming truth for us that *Jesus will return openly to our world, as King, and possibly soon; and then comes the glory of heaven* ...

So I pray that you will get excited about what you end up with from reading this book! But even more, that it deepens your longing for Christ!

Notes

[1] www.theguardian.com/world/2013/apr/02/americans-obama-anti-christ-conspiracy-theories (accessed 2nd March 2018).

[2] The Pew Research Center surveyed 2,196 evangelical leaders from 166 countries who were invited to attend the Third Lausanne Congress of World Evangelization in 2010 in Cape Town; 61 per cent said they believe in the 'rapture' of the Church – that as the end of the world draws near, Christians will be instantly taken up to heaven, leaving non-believers behind; 52 per cent said they believe that Jesus probably or definitely will return in their lifetime. Among leaders from the Global South, 67 per cent expected this in their lifetime, compared with 34 per cent from the Global North.

[3] The most respected statements even of the 'non-literal' approach at present seem to be Sam Storms' *Kingdom Come* (Mentor, 2013) and Kim Riddlebarger's *A Case For Amillennialism* (Baker, 2013), and both of these are American. I'm not being anti-American (that would be racist, and arguably it crops up often in the way we Brits reject ideas popular in the USA); but seriously, this British lack of interest isn't good.

[4] By the way, if you're reviewing this book, please don't describe its approach as 'dispensationalist'. It isn't. That word implies a whole other set of theories which aren't supported or even touched on here.

Chapter One

What's Clear First: Jesus Is Coming Back – What Does That Mean For Me?

Jesus will come back openly to earth as King. History as we know it will reach its end and climax. These are tremendously exciting and significant topics, and the Bible contains an enormous amount about them for us to explore. But practically first: what do they mean for us in real-life terms, right now?

One thing is sure: they mean *joy*! Not everything about Christ's return is clear, but let's start with what all Bible Christians are certain of, because it will fire up our hearts: Jesus really will return!

> This same Jesus, who has been taken from you into heaven, will come back in the same way you have seen him go into heaven.
> *Acts 1:11*

> For the Lord himself will come down from heaven, with a loud command, with the voice of the archangel and with the trumpet call of God,

and the dead in Christ will rise first. After that, we who are still alive and are left will be caught up together with them in the clouds to meet the Lord in the air. And so we will be with the Lord for ever!

1 Thessalonians 4:16-17

We don't know when, but this much is certain. History has an end. Human independence in rebellion against God has been a tragic, even catastrophic failure. At some point the agony has to stop. God looks at all the damage and hurt we've caused and says, 'Enough!'

We don't know when that will be: in fact, we know it will be at a time that we don't expect (Matthew 24:44). But we know the central things about *what* will happen. Jesus will return, in person, not to be born in a manger and crucified this time, but as the earth's King to finally put things right. *Amen!* Everything will be put right and there will be glory beyond our imaginations. Our human race's story has a good ending!

Grasp this and it will give us joy! Today there is so much fear about the future. Terrorist outrages: it's not *if* they will succeed in hitting us where it really hurts; it's when. Ecological breakdown: global warming, flooding, pollution. Economic struggles and unpredictability. Joblessness. Disease; superbugs. The world out of control. Where's it all going to end? We know! It's not that things *may* turn out OK. They *will* turn out OK. Jesus is in control and He loves us and He's coming back. Much of history is a disastrous mess, but it's not going nowhere. God will not tolerate the evil for ever.

That's why Jesus' return will happen. It has to. This is not a 'normal' world. It's a planet where the Fall has happened; where we've demanded our independence and ruined the world, and God has had to rescue it through the cross, resurrection and Pentecost. But still there's so much misery. Forty thousand children die each day of hunger and preventable disease. God loves people. There has to be an end to all the evil. History does have other purposes in the meantime, but there will come a time when God's goal in creating the eternal, global Church is complete, the gospel has spread to every nation and each culture is now represented gloriously in His eternal Bride; and God will tolerate the evil no longer. The end comes, everything is sorted out, and God's creation becomes what it was created to be!

And meanwhile, Jesus is saying, hang in. ('When the Son of Man comes, will he find faith on the earth?' [Luke 18:8]). God is faithful. Deliverance is coming. And from then on we will reign with Jesus for ever and ever!

Grasp that and it will indeed give you joy! But there's more. Look at Jesus' words in Matthew 24:42-50 and we'll see five vital facts:

1. Jesus' return will be *personal*, 24:42. It's *your* Lord who will come back. As Acts 1 says, the One who comes back is 'this same Jesus' that they already knew – and when He returns we will feel this too. Have you ever had the experience of finally meeting a friend or colleague whose personality you have known only by letter, and saying, 'It's you?' That's what we'll say: 'It's You! I've felt You at the edge of my senses, and in my deepest, most profound moments; and now it's You; You're here!'

2. Jesus' return will be *unexpected*, 24:44. Don't sit around waiting for signs, says Jesus. Yes, the population explosion, global warming and global pollution may make us think the end is near. Yes, some of what's happened with Israel in the last century may make us think that (as some people put it) the 'prophetic clock has started ticking again'. Yes, the gospel has almost spread to all nations, and we know when that has happened the End will come (24:14). But we really don't know just when. It really will happen when we don't expect it, says Jesus. So – to apply that exactly – it can happen today; at any moment. Maybe He will return today!

3. If we grasp this it will *change our lives*. This vision is essential for *holiness*, says Jesus (24:48-49). 2 Peter says the same: loss of vision for Christ's return goes with loss of vision for radical holiness (1:4 and 3:3-4). In 1 Peter 1:13-14, Peter makes a big emphasis on the choice of alternative desires we face, either of 'evil desires' or else desires for the glory to come 'when Jesus Christ is revealed'. Our hope is our anchor, says Hebrews 6:19. And it is: to grasp that Jesus is coming back for us in colossal glory changes our whole attitude to goals, to promotion, to investment, to bitterness, to forgiveness. So, Paul tells us, think about it, and especially when you take the bread and wine and declare Jesus' death for you, remember too that you're only doing this 'until he comes' (see what he says in 1 Corinthians 11:26)! It's 'to those who are waiting for him' that Jesus brings salvation (Hebrews 9:28; 1 Thessalonians 1:10). Reflect on this and give thanks for it (I would suggest) in your personal time with God at least once a week!

4. When Jesus returns there will be *judgement* (24:39). Talking about this is something very countercultural. But it's a fact, and it should fire us up to (as Paul says, 2 Corinthians 5:20) implore anyone we care about to be reconciled to the God they may soon stand before, while they still can! But there's also something here to challenge each of us. If you're a true Christian – if you've repented, made Jesus your Lord and put your faith in His death to pay for everything wrong and stupid you've done – then there's no question, you're going to heaven and not to hell. But there's something else that will happen (see v46): each of us will give an account of ourselves to God, as Romans 14:12 says. Why? Because God loves us and takes us seriously, and therefore He takes seriously what we do and how we live. And His Spirit is working hard to bring us to the point of 24:47 (the Master will put His servant 'in charge of all his possessions'[!!]), through everything that happens to us. And part of that is the accountability that leads to growth. Think of the best father you can possibly imagine, sitting with us and talking it through with us, saying to us, 'So tell me how it went': that's how it will be. And (because God the Holy Spirit is in every true believer, successfully making us more like Jesus), the end of this will be, as 1 Corinthians 4:5 amazingly expresses it, that each one of us will have *praise from God*. Imagine that!

And imagine also: this may happen on Tuesday next week (24:44)!

5. And then there will be colossal *glory*. The world will be brought back as God intended. Right now it's in bondage to decay (Romans 8:21); after Jesus returns, the wolf and the lamb will lie down together (look – I mean

23

now – at the fantastic passage in Isaiah 11:6-9), and the earth will be filled with the glory of God as the waters cover the sea! And (Matthew 24:47) *you* will be involved in looking after this! The eye has never seen what God has stored up for us (1 Corinthians 2:9). Perhaps more wonderfully still – because, as Dallas Willard says so perceptively, God is 'undoubtedly the most joyful being in the universe'[1] – He's going to invite you, us, to 'share' His 'happiness' (Matthew 25:21). Can you wait?

And those five facts are just the start. So much of the Bible is about the second coming. Let me end this chapter with four practical things; and may I suggest that (if you want this book to be in any way fruitful in your life) you stop now and turn them into prayer?

1. Grasp the facts of Jesus' return, and it will give you a passion for the lost. God's offer of salvation has a deadline (see 2 Corinthians 6:1-2 and Matthew 25:1-13). To say 'Not yet' to God is actually saying 'No' to Him as your Lord, because it's saying, 'This is my life and I'll do what I choose with it when I myself choose.' Are you doing that? The terrible thing is that one day God may accept what we say. It would be utter tragedy to wake up at last to how things really are, and then realise we've missed the deadline. That's why Paul says (2 Corinthians 5:20), 'We *implore* you … be reconciled to God' (emphasis mine)!

2. Grasp Jesus' return and it will give you a passion for distinctiveness. Our imagination is vital in this; the hope of our coming salvation is our helmet, says Paul in 1 Thessalonians 5: it protects our thinking. Our grasp of the heaven where we'll soon be going, the *priority* of heaven,

will help us towards a healthy detachment from overrating the issues of earth. 'Since everything will be destroyed in this way, what kind of people ought you to be?' asks Peter in 2 Peter 3:11. Jesus challenges us to lay up treasure that lasts, treasure in heaven, not on earth (Matthew 6:19-21). Career plans, money, possessions: grasping the second coming empowers us to hold these things loosely and not get too worked up about them. Glory is just around the corner; we will have a far better prize soon (Luke 16:11), and grasping that fact will help us not to be distracted away from the things that really count for the next million years!

3. That in turn will inspire us to use what we have now for the lost worldwide, for the needy worldwide, and for the kingdom and glory of God. Maybe it's good to read the second two stories in Matthew 25 in your personal time with God this coming week. They tell us about the Master who goes away and entrusts gifts and talents to His people, and then comes back and wants to know what they did with them. That's for us too. He will ask what we've done with what He's given us, for the lost, for the needy worldwide, and for His kingdom.

4. And most of all, grasping the second coming will enable us to do what Jesus tells us: Be ready! *Maybe today!* 'Keep watch because you do not know when the owner of the house will come back … If he comes suddenly, do not let him find you sleeping'! (Mark 13:35-36). To repeat, we will do well to reflect on this, briefly at least, in our personal time with God once each week. (And the first story in Matthew 25 – vv1-13 – is great for this.)

To summarise, then: Jesus' return will be personal; it will be sudden; it calls us to radical holiness, passionate witness and generous deployment of what God has entrusted to us till then; it will lead into our working through with our Father how we've lived here on earth; and from there onward to colossal glory!

Time to put this book down and pray, before we move on?

Notes

[1] From a marvellous passage about God in Dallas Willard, *The Divine Conspiracy* (Collins, 1998), p72.

Chapter Two

What Happens Next? And Might It Happen Soon?

Last chapter we explored the things to do with Jesus' return that we're sure of. From here on it gets more complex, but the questions are essential ones for us: *What will happen next? Does the Bible tell us much about the time before Jesus comes back as King? And might it happen soon?*

(And for those of us who prefer the theological term: What's all this stuff about the coming 'tribulation'? Or for fans of Ireland's greatest twentieth-century poet, W B Yeats in 'The Second Coming':

> And what rough beast, its hour come round at last,
> Slouches towards Bethlehem to be born?)[1]

The day of the Animal

The answer to question two above seems to be, Yes; Scripture really does have plenty to say about the time before Jesus comes back as King, and we should seek to learn all we can from it. The Bible seems to say that, before

Jesus finally intervenes, there will be a brief period in which humankind learns the full horrendous consequences of what it means to live lives independent from God. In Matthew 24:3 Jesus has been asked, 'What will be the sign of your coming?', and He responds by speaking of wars, famines and earthquakes, then says that 'All these are the beginning of birth-pains' (v8). In other words, there's huge glory to come when He returns, but there's a seriously bad time along the way.

This is one of the things the book of Revelation is about (besides, vitally, equipping us to 'overcome', to handle pressure in every generation), and we need to take it seriously. As we read Revelation from chapter 8 through to Jesus' triumphant appearance at the end of chapter 19 – and to get a grip on all this we should do so; it's only ten pages! – it's impossible not to feel we are being warned: before Jesus reappears, things will get very dark indeed. We wanted our independence from God, a world free of God; and God has been restraining evil and protecting us from the full consequences of that choice. But for a very short time, in the final phase of history, He gives us what we have desired and allows our race to learn what rejecting God's rule really means, to experience the full terrible consequences of living without God. It is bad; in fact, Jesus says that it will be 'great distress, unequalled from the beginning of the world until now – and never to be equalled again', and that unless God had strictly limited this period, 'no-one would survive' (Matthew 24:21-22).[2]

Revelation paints the picture unflinchingly: horrific slaughter in global warfare (look at 9:13-16; 16:14; 6:1-4), a poisoned world (look at 8:11; 16:3-4), famine (6:8), natural disaster (look at 16:8-9), disease (6:8; 16:2,11) and economic exploitation (6:5-6; 18:1-20). (The technical term for this horrendous period is the 'tribulation' ['*the* great tribulation', Revelation 7:14].) Remember, we are talking about reading these chapters with a more 'literal' understanding, but it isn't so clear what they're saying if we read them otherwise (and I suspect therefore that churches taught to read them more 'non-literally' can tend not to read them too often).[3]

And then there is the part that is most well known: totalitarian dictatorship leading to horrific persecution (look at Revelation 13). Satan suffers some crucial defeat in the supernatural world (12:9) and, knowing that history is coming to a climax, raises up the ultimate evil ruler (13:1-2). In popular parlance this individual is called the antichrist. (I've been intrigued to find my Muslim friends using this term for the end-time evil leader that their own prophetic traditions lead them to expect: the Dajjal, who they believe will be defeated and killed by Jesus when He returns.) 'Antichrist', however, isn't the biblical term; in fact, the New Testament uses that for anyone who is anti-Christ (1 John 2:18; 2 John 7). Revelation's term for the end-time dictator (eg in 13:5,17; 14:9; 19:19-20) is perhaps best translated 'the Animal'.

The persecution the Animal unleashes on the people of God, indeed on anyone who opposes him, is horrific. 'All who refused to worship the image' of the Animal are killed; and he forces 'everyone, small and great, rich and poor, free and slave, to receive a mark on his right hand or on his forehead, so that no-one could buy or sell unless he had the mark, which is the name of the beast [the Animal] or the number of his name' (Revelation 13:16-17). The technology of an increasingly cashless, credit-chip society could make this all very easy to begin with. The authorities would express regret: your credit line is currently cut off, your grocery and electricity and medical bills are not being paid, and obviously you cannot run up further expenditure. Eventually, since you cannot pay your local property taxes, you lose your house. And all because of your intransigence on a minor matter of worship! Life could become increasingly impossible for whole families, yet very cleanly and with no unpleasant violence or brutality. At least, that is how it might start; it would not be how it ends.

If all this were only told to us in the apocalyptic book of Revelation, we might wonder how to take it. But look at how Paul talks about the final dictator in the context of a normal letter, 2 Thessalonians 2:1-9. Here Paul explains that a key feature of the period immediately preceding Christ's second coming will be the rise of a satanically inspired individual who 'will oppose and will exalt himself over everything that is called God or is worshipped, so that he sets himself up in God's temple, proclaiming himself to be God'. (It is striking to see in vv5-6 that Paul had seen it as a priority to explain these matters to the young Christians in Thessalonica during his very brief visit there: he may have been there no more than three weeks.)

2 Thessalonians certainly isn't a book that can be classed as 'wildly apocalyptic'. For me this is a major reason for taking the 'tribulation' and the Animal very literally. (And the fact that strong proponents of the 'non-literal' approach, such as Kim Riddlebarger and Sam Storms, also

foresee the rise of this ultimately evil end-time dictator[4] should be an added reminder to take this prospect very seriously.)

The information God gives us in these parts of the New Testament is tantalising, and we may well want to know more. How will we know *when* it's upon us? In the passage we have just quoted, Paul seems to be highlighting, as the climax of this individual's evil and the key warning point that the End has come, a moment when he desecrates God's temple by entering it and demanding worship there. And we may well see a parallel with Matthew 24:15, where Jesus warns that the crucial sign to look out for, indicating that all hell is about to break loose and His people should take to the hills, is 'when you see standing in the holy place the "abomination that causes desolation"'. Right now, of course, no such temple or 'holy place' exists in Jerusalem. Some writers (particularly those with a strong anti-Catholic bent) have noted the possible parallels to Ephesians 2:21 and 1 Corinthians 3:16-17, and seen this 'temple' as God's Church. But then whatever could Paul be describing when he speaks of the Animal 'setting himself up in God's temple', since biblically the word 'Church' means the invisible, supernatural, universal Bride of Christ, and not any earthly social institution such as the Catholic Church or the Church of England?

In contrast, back in the second century AD, Hippolytus saw this as a Jewish temple, replacing the one destroyed by the Romans in AD70; so did Cyril of Jerusalem two centuries later.[5] And this is more probable, surely, since the Jewish temple is clearly the 'holy place' that Jesus refers to in Matthew 24:15, and is equally clearly the subject of the

Daniel references (presumably 9:27 and 12:11) to which Matthew explicitly links Jesus' words.[6] That rebuilt Jewish temple doesn't yet exist; but let's hold that question over to the next chapter, where it will become important as we consider the vital issue: Will we Christians still be on earth during this horrific period at all?

Another – rather practical – question that has fascinated many ordinary Christians is *where* and from what part of the world will the Animal come? This is the kind of question that really annoys some academics, but the fact is that God has chosen for a surprising amount of Scripture to describe the international politics of the end time (see, almost certainly, the closing section of Daniel 11, which presents geopolitical events that haven't occurred in history thus far; likewise Ezekiel 38 and 39 about the invader from the 'far north' attacking Israel;[7] likewise Revelation 16:12). That being so, a gentle interest in end-time geopolitics seems legitimate – except that these are presumably passages that will only become clear when the time comes. It might not seem unreasonable to wonder whether the Animal will have something to do with Europe, or at least Rome, since when Daniel 9:26 prophesies the destruction of Jerusalem and the temple after the 'cutting off' of Christ, the destroyers are 'the people of the ruler who will come', and they of course were the Romans. Similarly, Revelation 17:7-9 links the Animal with 'seven hills', and any educated person at the time when Revelation was written would have made the link with Rome, which was famously built on seven hills.[8] (Still, I gather that Sheffield is too. Speculation may be intriguing in these matters, but dogmatism is highly unwise!)

But one practical thing is very important about this awesome final period, when the implications of our alienation from God are made terribly clear. As it describes the unleashing of one evil after another, Revelation continually repeats phrases like 'he was given' (6:2,4 [twice],8; 7:2; 9:1,3,5; 13:5,7 [twice]; 16:8). God is allowing the powers of evil free rein, but only for a brief, specific period. Jesus in Matthew 24:21-22 emphasises that this period is limited; and over and over again elsewhere its length is carefully stated, in three equivalent phrases: 1,260 days, forty-two months, 'a time, times, and half a time' (ie, presumably, three and a half years). (See Revelation 11:2,3; 12:6,14; 13:5; also Daniel 7:25; 9:27; 12:7,11.)

Are these time-limits literal or symbolic? It's very hard to see that 1,260 or forty-two have any obvious symbolic meanings for the reader, so the natural way to view them is as describing a very specific, literal and *limited* period; particularly since Jesus Himself has flagged up the idea of this desperate time having strict limits from God.[9] (This, however – the fact that forty-two and 1,260 are hard to understand if not literally – becomes another reason for reading the passages we have discussed here in a fairly literal way overall.)

One major goal of Revelation seems to be to give a discipleship manual strengthening God's people to be 'overcomers' in pressure, whether in the first century, the period since or the end time; and the truth that strengthens us here is that even the supreme example of evil will not be able to pressurise us one day longer than God allows. Whenever God finally says 'Enough!', it will be.

So we should worship (I mean, now!)! Even when evil is at its most rampant, Jesus is Lord!

So, might we live through this? Might it happen soon?

When will this climax of history come?

The most important answer is: We don't know. 'No-one knows about that day or hour, not even the angels in heaven, nor the Son, but only the Father', Jesus warned (Matthew 24:36). 'Therefore keep watch, because you do not know on what day your Lord will come ... be ready, because the Son of Man will come at an hour when you do not expect him' (vv42,44).

We need to be careful: there are apparent signs that can deceive us into a false expectancy, particularly at times of global crisis (vv3-6). And that has often happened. A century ago many Christians saw Mussolini's attempt to revive the Roman Empire as a clear sign of the end, and they were wrong; many Russian believers jumped to the same conclusion over President Gorbachev (because of the mark on his head) and Chernobyl (which some Russian dictionaries translated into English as 'wormwood', as in Revelation 8:11). Ronald Reagan apparently remarked about events in Libya that, 'For the first time ever, everything is in place for the battle of Armageddon and the second coming of Christ';[10] and while he was President of the USA he wrote to the mayor of Jerusalem:

> You know, I turn back to your ancient prophets
> in the Old Testament and the signs foretelling
> Armageddon, and I find myself wondering ... if

we're the generation to see that come about. I
don't know if you've noted any of these
prophecies lately but, believe me, they certainly
describe the times we're going through.[11]

(Apparently *The Guardian* added, reporting this, 'Have a
nice day yourself, Ronnie.') There have been many other
examples throughout history, and as they fall away, one
after another, they bring the Bible and the Church into
disrepute.

And yet that's not quite the whole story. Jesus also told
His disciples, 'Now learn this lesson from the fig tree: As
soon as its twigs get tender and its leaves come out, you
know that summer is near. Even so, when you see all these
things, you know that it is near, right at the door' (Matthew
24:32-33). 'These things' are the signs of Matthew 24 (which
is why we need to understand them as best we can); but
His words demonstrate that the question 'Will all this
happen soon?' is a legitimate one, even though we need to
be cautious with our answers.

As we look at the pressures of global warming,
increasing pollution, population explosion and much
more, we may well feel that things cannot go on as they
are, and the climax when God says 'Enough!' may not be
far away. The chief economist of the International Energy
Agency warned recently that our world is currently
heading for six degrees of global warming this century, an
outcome he said would be catastrophic (and that some
scientists have argued will bring about our extinction). The
population explosion which preoccupied many earlier
futurologists no longer commands the headlines, but this
isn't because the problem has been solved, rather because

it has proven to be too difficult. The United Nations foresees the world population being 11.2 billion – the present number plus half as much again – late in the twenty-first century.[12] It is hard to imagine what a world containing 11 billion people will be like, but we probably need to try. In recent decades the world for the first time began to need more food than it grew; and each year nearly 100 million more people are being added to its population. The World Commission on Water likewise reported that within twenty-five years we will need 56 per cent more water than is currently available, leading perhaps to water wars. 'We are sawing through the branch that is holding us,' said a UN report on world population, 'and if we carry on as before, it may break and bring us crashing down with it … We are not talking about the interests of distant descendants. It is our own children.'[13]

The direction of our Western culture's spiritual development (which after all is its most important feature) may point us gently towards similar conclusions. It's not hard to see, in the evolution of our literature, art and music, our philosophy and ethics, the tragic implosion, one after another, of the 'god-substitutes' with which we've tried to fill the gap in our culture's foundations left by the God we've rejected: reason, in the period we call the Enlightenment; then the very different gods of Romanticism; then the gods – or idols – of science, art for its own sake, and relationships ('All You Need is Love', to quote The Beatles), in which we placed our faith until modernity began to draw to a close. And here we are now in postmodernity, sceptical of all big-picture 'meta-narratives', doubtful whether there are any real values that can give us identity and self-worth and our lives meaning and direction; and perhaps most significantly, having no real basis for that confidence in the reality of right and wrong, and no real counterweight for self-interest, without which our communities will descend towards the law of the jungle.[14]

Of course there have been 'dark ages' in history before. But these did not occur at a time of overpopulation and environmental crisis, or of terrorists armed perhaps with biological or nuclear weapons. The forces that then assumed control were pre-civilised, rather than from cultures marked by the collapse of faith in any ethics at all. Now, however, our all-conquering Western media are successfully exporting our individualism, our materialism and our collapse of values throughout the world, along with our hamburgers, cola and jeans. It seems probable that neither the Confucian-based family values of east Asia, the communal values of traditional African culture, nor even the Islamic values of the Middle East, are doing very well in the battle with the web and the satellite dish for the soul of the rising generation; Ronald McDonald marches irresistibly onward. This in no way proves that we have reached the end times; and yet perhaps there is increasingly a 'sense of an ending' to our world's spiritual history.

And even without the looming environmental disaster, it is all too easy to see our future as one where law and order have collapsed along with their underlying ethics. (This was the experience in the Soviet Union after the reign of communism fell apart and was replaced by that of the ubiquitous mafia.) God makes clear in His Word that rebelling against Him leads us into the hands of evil. Freedom is not something inevitable and automatic in a liberal society: it is where the Son sets us free that we are free indeed (John 8:36; 2 Corinthians 3:17). So turning away from God means in the long run being given over to evil, and that means losing our freedom.

We see it starting to happen: the loss of God leads to a loss of ethics, which leads in turn to cynicism about democracy and leadership. It's hard to see democracy thriving in a post-God culture that is both under threat and also sceptical as to whether ethics really exist or beliefs can have any certainty, and therefore whether elections are any more than tournaments for rival advertising agencies; where there is an increasing sense of ghettoisation, of different interest groups competing nakedly for position and power; and indeed where postmodernist thinkers are preaching openly that with God dead, ethics beyond discussion and truth unattainable, the universal struggle for power is all that really exists. Plus, with technological progress towards cashlessness in particular, possibilities now exist for a totalitarian regime to shore up its control in the ways we find in Revelation 13:17, far more than ever before.[15] In a highly pressured society, social control can be deeply attractive if it promises reduction of crime. Again, none of this proves that the End is near; but what Revelation does tell us is that our rebellion will one day climax in the emergence of a final dictator; and the environment in which the emergence of the Animal could make sense is clearly coming into being.

There are at least two other issues. Since 1948 Israel has been back in its land as a nation for the first time since its expulsion in AD135 (something Bible prophecies had led Christians to be looking for since at least the 1820s).[16] It is very hard for our own generation to grasp the impact of this astonishing event: Israel as a nation had been missing from the global map since the remote depths of antiquity, and with its re-emergence many Christians had a sense that the 'prophetic clock had started ticking again', and the end times could not be far away. Seven decades later, that argument cannot have the same force; but perhaps it is not negligible.

But for me personally, the most striking insight in all this is one I owe to Nigel Lee, formerly the deeply respected campus ministry leader of UCCF, the student Christian Union movement in Britain. Jesus said the gospel will be preached 'to all nations, and then the end will come' (Matthew 24:14), bringing about the completion of the global Bride of Christ that is a key purpose of history (Revelation 7:9). With the staggering growth of God's Church all around the world in the last century, it's very hard to see this process needing more than another hundred years, probably less.[17] And once it is completed, said Jesus, the End will come. In that case, very possibly either we or our children's generation need to be prepared for the climax of history that Revelation describes.

If this is a genuine possibility (and hopefully friends who take a different view will recognise that the possibility exists), then it's best to face up to it. In particular, this means we must cultivate a Christianity that is not consumerist, not one we follow for our own therapy or just because it makes us feel good. One day it may not! The reason we follow Jesus is that His gospel is *true* – and in the end our response to it will lead us to an eternity in either heaven or hell. Our prayer must be: *Lord, I will live by following You, and if need be I pray that You give me the strength to die for You.* The apostle Peter wrote:

> Dear friends, do not be surprised at the painful trial you are suffering, as though something strange were happening to you. But rejoice that you participate in the sufferings of Christ, so that you may be overjoyed when his glory is revealed.
> *1 Peter 4:12-13*

How would we live now if we *knew* that would be our situation in ten years' time? Our answer will tell us a lot about how much we love Jesus. The sensible thing is to prepare ourselves for the possibility;[18] if we or our kids might be the 'hero generation' called to live through this, we'd better get trained...

And let's be clear: that training will pay huge dividends in other situations too – just as meditating on the themes of Revelation will do – because 'days of evil' (see Ephesians 6:13) do come to each of us from time to time. In this world we will have trouble, said Jesus (John 16:33); in our family sometimes, in our workplace too.

Reading *In God's Underground*, Richard Wurmbrand's hugely inspirational story of persecution in communist Romania, helped me enormously as a young Christian. I read of the incredible pressures he survived, and couldn't help thinking that I shouldn't complain about what happened in my own life. God does strengthen the weak (Hebrews 4:16). Reading Revelation and being aware of the possible coming of the Animal will help us cope with pressure, will help us cope with inconveniences now; and, just possibly, it will also one day give us the guts to take our place in the hero generation, and 'after you have done everything, to stand' (Ephesians 6:13) for God.

But then again, perhaps this is not what will happen at all. What about the 'rapture'?

Notes

1 Excerpt from W B Yeats, `The Second Coming`, Copyright ©
Caitriona Yeats. Used with express permission of United
Agents on behalf of Caitriona Yeats.

2 Surely this verse makes it very hard to see this part of
Matthew 24 as limited to AD70, as some interpreters suggest.

3 I say 'more literal': it would presumably be obvious to any
sensible reader that, while the Animal might be an absolutely
literal dictator, his 'seven heads' in 13:1 would be metaphorical,
like those in the dream-visions of Daniel, rather than literal –
but to make that quite clear they are given an interpretation in
17:9-10. Again, 'Babylon', so central to chapters 17 and 18,
seems from 1 Peter 5:13 to be contemporary slang not for literal
Babylonia but for literal Rome. But it isn't obvious why war,
famine and dictatorship need mean anything but literal war,
famine and dictatorship.

4 See Kim Riddlebarger in *A Case for Amillennialism* (eg
pp146,155,272) and Sam Storms in *Kingdom Come* (pp536,546-
47).

5 'What temple then? He means, the Temple of the Jews which
has been destroyed. For God forbid that it should be the one in
which we are! Why say we this? That we may not be supposed
to favour ourselves. For if he [the end-time satanic dictator]
comes to the Jews as Christ, and desires to be worshipped by
the Jews, he will make great account of the Temple, that he may
more completely beguile them; making it supposed that he is
the man of the race of David, who shall build up the Temple
which was erected by Solomon. And Antichrist will come at the
time when there shall not be left one stone upon another in the
Temple of the Jews, according to the doom pronounced by our
Saviour' (Cyril of Jerusalem, Catechetical Lecture 15).

[6] But whether the temple is to be understood as a literal temple still to be rebuilt in Jerusalem, or (somehow) the 'temple' of God's Church, Paul's presentation of this as the key moment in the rise of the ultimate evil end-time individual seems to parallel Matthew 24:14-16 so clearly that one of two things surely follows. Either we must understand Matthew 24:14-16 as being about the end times, not (just) about AD70, as is sometimes suggested. Or, we must think of the key events of history as having a spiral, foreshadowing character – which is exactly what many of the 'literalists' say about the puzzling relationship of Matthew 24 and Luke 21. More about all this in Appendix A.

[7] Here, interestingly, the Septuagint, the Greek Old Testament translation that Christ and the apostles used and quoted, describes the leader of this invasion from the 'far north' as the 'prince of Rosh' (38:2 and 39:1); see also the NIV margin. Might this be Russia?

[8] Hal Lindsey's huge bestseller *The Late Great Planet Earth*, written in the 1970s heyday of the Jesus Movement and described by *The New York Times* as the 'no.1 non-fiction bestseller of the decade', offered a wide range of speculations about the geopolitics of the end-time and how they might fulfil prophecies such as Daniel 11 and Ezekiel 38. It's actually still worth getting from Amazon: some of his proposals may one day turn out to be right. Anyway, here's one that Lindsey missed: 'Europa' was originally a woman in Greek mythology who is usually pictured riding an animal (Zeus embodied as a bull). This image has been used in various ways in European Union contexts, and is for example the theme of a sculpture outside the European council building in Brussels. The strong parallel between the woman riding the animal in Revelation 17:3 and this Europa has not gone unnoticed by those who study these things… Whether Europe would become the heartland of the Animal was a significant election issue when

Norway was voting whether to join the European Community.

9 We should note too that when Daniel himself is interpreting a prophecy involving seventy years in Daniel 9:2-3, he clearly takes that seventy absolutely literally.

10 articles.latimes.com/1988-01-03/opinion/op-32475_1_president-reagan (accessed 2nd March 2018).

11 www.notable-quotes.com/r/reagan_ronald_iii.html (accessed 2nd March 2018).

12 *World Population Prospects: The 2017 Revision,* published in June 2017 by the UN Department of Economic and Social Affairs.

13 Source unavailable.

14 There are hugely important issues here which help us see why it's inane to say, as so many people do, 'You believe in God, and I don't, and it doesn't really matter either way'. If we really understand our 'loss of God' we'll see that it's the key factor underlying many of our culture's most serious pressure points. It matters enormously whether He's there or not! For a full survey see Pete Lowman, *A Long Way East of Eden* (2001), accessible online at http://www.bethinking.org/god/a-long-way-east-of-eden, particularly chapter 6; or more briefly http://www.bethinking.org/your-studies/western-literature-and-the-death-of-god (accessed 2nd March 2018).

15 We are now much closer to a cashless society where all transactions are underwritten by 'smart card', or indeed by body parts. The savings for the banking system could be enormous. But if everything is bought or sold in this way, then our individual behaviour and activities can be tracked very extensively. Yet the idea is so efficient and cost-effective that is hard not to envisage it becoming fairly universal in the developed world sooner or later.

[16] W H Harding's biography of George Müller records how, in the 1820s, war broke out between Russia and the Turkish Empire that controlled Palestine, 'and many good, excellent Christians said, "*Now* the Turkish Empire will be destroyed and Israel will be restored"' (*The Life of George Muller* [Oliphants, n.d.], p329). They were wrong about the timing; it took another 120 years. But arguably they were right about God's promises and His rule over history.

[17] This vision was a major passion when the student Christian Union movements arose in the English-speaking world; 'Evangelize to a Finish to Bring Back the King' was the watchword devised by Howard Guinness, the British Christian Union leader whom God used in the formation of the evangelical student movements in Canada, Australia and New Zealand.

[18] One route to survival (as in the earlier European dark ages) would no doubt be in small communities deeply committed to shared values, and deeply committed and supportive to each other, based together on the rediscovery of the empowering of the supernatural (particularly in prayer) and seeking together to be sources of renewal or sanity for the wider community around them. This passage from 1 Peter has helpful counsel for communities facing the prospect of apocalyptic collapse: 'The end of all things is near. Therefore be clear minded and self-controlled so that you can pray. Above all, love each other deeply, because love covers over a multitude of sins. Offer hospitality to one another without grumbling. Each one should use whatever gift he has received to serve others' (4:7-10). These are key ingredients for communities seeking to survive amid social disintegration: clear Bible-shaped thinking; disciplined determination; release of God's power into their situation by prayer; commitment to deep mutual love, with a broader degree of mutual forgiveness than might be called for in less-difficult circumstances; and availability of the resources and

talents of each member to the needs of every other, building on the assumption that because there is a Holy Spirit, each member has an ability and a contribution to make.

Chapter Three

So Where Will We Be During The Final Crisis? What's This About The 'Rapture'?

So let's recap. The final crisis of history arrives. Before Christ returns as King, God briefly allows humankind the independence from His control that we've wanted, and to see the full consequences of what it means to live lives fully separate from God. With no divine restraint left, evil, unhindered, bears fruit in a poisoned world, in extremes of disease, famine and natural disaster, along with global war and dire totalitarianism. And is this soon? Possibly. There is a real possibility that we or our children may be called to be the 'hero generation'.

Or we may not. Apparently the majority of Bible Christians worldwide see it very differently. So here's the question for this chapter: Will we as believers live through the final crisis or not? (In theological terms: What's all that stuff about the 'rapture', and is it credible?) Here Christians disagree. There's lots about this that Scripture doesn't make clear, perhaps deliberately.

The crucial passage about the 'rapture' is 1 Thessalonians 4:16-17, which describes Christ's return, 'the coming of the Lord' (v15). Here it is:

> For the Lord himself will come down from heaven, with a loud command, with the voice of the archangel and with the trumpet call of God, and the dead in Christ will rise first. After that, we who are still alive and are left will be caught up together with them in the clouds to meet the Lord in the air. And so we will be with the Lord for ever.[1]

And our minds can move on from there to what the angels in Acts 1:11 promised the disciples who had watched Christ leave them and ascend back to heaven: 'This same Jesus, who has been taken from you into heaven, will come back in the same way you have seen him go into heaven.' When He does, all who are believers and on earth at that time will suddenly be 'caught up in the clouds' and will be with Him in glory beyond our imaginations forever! *(Thank You, Lord!)*

This much is marvellously clear. There is, however, a problem if we start to look at the details of the timing. Passages like Matthew 24:36,42-44 seem to present Christ's future coming as a completely unexpected event erupting into history: 'The Son of Man will come at an hour when you do not expect him.' In contrast, some of the passages we've considered in the previous chapter describe a very difficult period before He returns, specifically limited to 1,260 days or three and a half years, which will contain plenty of pointers that His second coming is near. (But that would imply that we believers live through this period.)

Bible Christians treat this problem in at least three different ways.

1. Brothers and sisters who see the prophetic passages in more 'non-literal' terms, and so see the references to this frequently described, horrific 1,260-day period as somehow symbolic, may say that the problem only arises if we press the Bible text into an inappropriately exact precision. But this book is designed to set out the approach that takes all these passages fairly literally – and, for me at least, these approaches are vindicated by the fact that they make interesting sense of so many passages that are obscure, hence often almost ignored, in the 'non-literal' approach. Within the more 'literal' approaches, however, there are at least two further options.

2. Many Christians believe that Christ's second coming is in fact in two phases, and that the Bible is saying that we believers will never pass through this horrendous time. First, at any moment, at a moment when we don't expect (Matthew 24:44), God will take His people out to be with Himself. The 'rapture' is the technical term for this, and it's what 1 Thessalonians 4:15-18 describes, and possibly Matthew 24:36-42 too. Christ takes all His people away; and only then, with all true Christian input and restraint removed (the preservative 'salt of the earth' that arrests decay, Matthew 5:13), and with God ceasing to hold back the disastrous consequences of our insistence on our autonomy, will all hell briefly break loose on earth. 2 Thessalonians 2:6-8 speaks of the end-time satanic dictator and says:

You know what is holding him back, so that he may be revealed at the proper time. For the secret power of lawlessness is already at work; but the one who now holds it back will continue to do so till he is taken out of the way. And then the lawless one will be revealed, whom the Lord Jesus will overthrow with the breath of his mouth and destroy by the splendour of his coming.

In this understanding, the removal of 'the one who now holds it back' means – and personally I haven't found any alternative very plausible[2] – the removal of the Spirit's influence through His people.[3] This finally creates a situation where evil can break loose unhindered, until eventually God says, 'Enough', and comes back openly to reign on earth.

Imagine; it's all too easy to see how removal of the 'salt' would have that effect. If everyone truly living Jesus' way were to be pulled out of business, politics, economics, the media, the world's religious systems, the police, it's not surprising if all hell were to break loose. And if this 'removal' could happen at any moment, that too is a very powerful thought. If we've accepted Christ and His forgiveness and lordship, we will be rescued 'from the coming wrath' (1 Thessalonians 1:10); if not – well, it's not clever to get left behind to face the final agony of history. And as Jesus says in Matthew 24, it will happen when we don't expect. *('But at least it won't happen tonight!'* Precisely.) So God snatches His people out before the 'wrath' comes; the final crisis doesn't happen till Jesus' people – and their influence – are gone. And therefore there is no sign to say 'The End is near': we simply 'do not know the day or the hour' when Jesus will take us (Matthew 25:13). In contrast, as the final crisis proceeds there will be plenty of signs that the second phase, Christ's coming *openly* as King, is 'near, right at the door', when finally He is going to take full control and say 'Enough!' to all the evil (Matthew 24:22,33).

3. The third understanding is that Christ's second coming consists of only one event, at the very *end* of the 1,260 days; but that event does begin with Christ's persecuted followers being caught up to meet Him and coming back *immediately* with Him, visibly vindicated as His beloved people.[4] Then the Bible verses about it happening at a time when we don't expect are God's warning that it's all too easy to miss the signs.

So there are various possibilities. What then would the rapture, the sudden disappearance of all true believers, be like? Books like LaHaye's *Left Behind* series have had a field day describing planes crashing because the pilot has suddenly been taken to heaven, motorway pile-ups caused by cars whose drivers have vanished, family members coming home to find that parents or (especially) children have totally disappeared. Or long before LaHaye, Larry Norman was the #1 bard to the Jesus Movement, which made a huge impact for the gospel on Western youth culture when the 1960s hippie dreams were fading.[5] In his most well-known song, 'I Wish We'd All Been Ready',[6] based on Matthew 24:36-42, he embodies the experience of suddenly realising that your spouse or companion has been taken, disappeared, and you yourself are left; that your life choices about Jesus have now become catastrophically permanent…

Why believe in the rapture?

Besides the passages just quoted, what are the key reasons for believing in a 'rapture' coming *before* the final crisis (the 'pre-trib' position, to quote the popular shorthand)? To my mind there are eight at least that are thought-provoking (and another is included in this chapter's endnotes), particularly in the way they resolve some puzzling enigmas in the biblical text. Some of these are slightly technical, but they matter because it matters whether the 'next big event' we live expecting is our sudden departure to be with Christ in glory forever, or (first) the coming to power of the Animal. So see what you think...

1. Christians believing in a 'pre-trib' rapture remind us of Jesus' teaching that the 'next big event' will occur suddenly, when we least expect it (look at Matthew 24:44). However, the catastrophes and persecutions described in Revelation will clearly herald the End to the godly people enduring them (see also Matthew 24:33: 'When you see all these things, you know that it is near, right at the door'). It's hard to imagine that believers who live through those events would find the Lord's coming in glory so unexpected. (History actually suggests the opposite, that when believers come under pressure, we are usually all too quick to assume that the Lord's coming is imminent.) Indeed, in the light of God's repeated words about 1,260 days or forty-two months being the length of the final crisis, we can imagine those desperately persecuted believers having the blessing of being able to guess with some accuracy when Jesus their Rescuer will come.[7] (And Matthew 24:32-33 could seem to be encouraging them to do so.)

So how do we explain the very sudden shift from the predictability of Matthew 24:33 to the unforeseen coming of verse 44? On the one hand, verse 33 indeed says Christ's followers should sense 'these things', the climax of history, coming. But the following verses, particularly verses 38-41, seem to present people living in a more 'normal' life situation, and therefore emphasise repeatedly that the second coming, 'that day', will happen exactly when they aren't expecting it.[8] It's hard, therefore, to see those verses as referring to exactly the same event or the same time as the 'great distress' of verses 15-22: if such unprecedented horrors are taking place, will Jesus' disciples ('you', v44) really have no sense of His impending return? The simple explanation is that verses 36-44 are describing the rapture and the time before it, and that these prophetic verses will be fulfilled *before* the very obvious 'great distress' of verses 15-22, after which Christ returns openly. So the 'pre-trib' argument, that these verses describe a period before both the rapture and the tribulation, has some real force. The problem disappears: verses 30-33 are referring to Christ's open return in glory and the events that will happen before it, and verses 36-44 to the earlier, unforeseeable 'coming of the Son of Man', the rapture, when one will be taken and the other left (vv40-41); when (like Noah, v37) God's people are taken out to safety before the judgement comes. Logically, then, it makes sense that the world-shaking finish of the carefully numbered 1,260 days, with Jesus' final victorious and (24:33) not unpredictable return in glory, is a quite separate and distinct event from the 'coming of the Son of Man' described in verses 36-44, which we can't foresee and don't expect. (And for us now, therefore, the unexpected event Jesus speaks of in vv36-44 is the 'next big one'.)

It is of course true that in this case Jesus is not spelling out the relationship between this event and His open return. Instead, the disciples are being presented with a complex 'mystery' (cf 1 Corinthians 15:51 talking about the same event) that will be clarified later; just as Old Testament prophecies like Isaiah 61:2 or Zechariah 9:9-13 sometimes have an unexplained complexity as they combine allusions to both Christ's first and second comings, which likewise turned out to be separate events.[9]

2. This – our deliverance in the rapture coming before the 'tribulation' – would also explain why the emphasis of the famous parables with which Jesus follows His great discourse on the end times in Matthew 24 is not, 'Gear up and prepare yourselves for the coming savage persecution,' but, 'Be ready and prepared for your Master's unexpected return.' That does seem to be what He is presenting in these parables as the next major event.

Importantly, we find the same in the words of 1 Thessalonians 5 about the 'day of the Lord', the horrific time at the end of history. Here, too, Paul's emphasis is not on cultivating the faithfulness and unshakeability that will be needed in a future time of horrendous trial, but on 'being alert' right now. Indeed, 1 Thessalonians 5:9 tells us explicitly that 'God did not appoint us to suffer wrath' (Jesus' coming from heaven 'rescues us from the coming wrath', 1:10); and we might think that Paul is referring there to the last judgement and hell, until we notice that this promise's context in chapter 5 is most probably (vv1-4) the destruction that happens on earth in the end-time 'day of the Lord'.[10] We won't face the 'wrath' of that terrible final crisis of history, Paul may well seem to be saying, because Jesus will come back first and take us up to be with Him before it happens.[11] We're 'not in darkness' (v4) in the sense of being unsaved and outside Christ, and therefore in God's mercy we won't be left behind. So then the (pre-trib) rapture described in the immediately preceding verses (4:15-18) is why Paul can say, 'Therefore *encourage* one another with these words' (4:18, emphasis mine); it's our 'hope of salvation', of deliverance and rescue (5:8); encourage one another (5:11) in the light of that deliverance, rather than gearing up for massive persecution.

3. A more minor enigma: It's somewhat odd, if the rapture happens as a dramatic, 'post-tribulation' deliverance where God's people are snatched out right at the climax and end of the 1,260 days of unequalled distress – somewhere around the time of Revelation 6:12, for example, or 16:16, or particularly before their triumphant reappearance in glory in 19:11 – that it's not clearly described in any of these.

(But there are possible answers to that. Could Revelation 14:14-16 be hinting at a rapture right at the end of the tribulation, coming as it does not long before the book's narrative doubles back to start a new section in 15:1?[12] Or, if Jesus' warning comparing His return to the coming of a thief (Matthew 24:43-44) refers to the rapture, might not the rapture likewise be in view when He says 'Behold, I come like a thief!' in Revelation 16:15, just before the final battle (v16) and the End (v20)? Are these passages at least hints of a 'post-trib rapture' in Revelation?)

4. Another minor enigma that the 'pre-trib' approach resolves is that whenever the rapture occurs ('pre-trib' or 'post-trib'), it seems to involve Christ's followers being caught up from the earth to meet Him in the air, leaving behind all those whose unbelief has left them trapped in the final horror. But in Christ's words about the 'end of the age' in Matthew 13:40-43, He seems to be bothering to make clear that then things will be the other way round: the angels are sent out to 'weed out', take away, the wicked *'first'* (see also 13:30); it is the righteous who are left behind for the 'kingdom' time that will follow (v43). This again suggests that the rapture of 1 Thessalonians 4 and the absolute 'end of the age' of Matthew 13 are two separate events.

5. Now a larger-scale issue. On the one hand the New Testament often seems to emphasise that the Lord may come for us at any moment: 'The Judge is standing at the door!'(James 5:9). But then there also seem to be some things that have to happen before the Lord returns in glory, which implies that we can know that that return in glory won't happen quite yet. However, if the rapture and Christ's open return in glory are two separate events, so that those things happen in between them, this is another enigma solved.

Let's give two examples. As we saw in the previous chapter, Paul, writing in a calm, thoroughly non-apocalyptic way in 2 Thessalonians 2:3-4, presents as a crucial sign of the End the final dictator coming to power and setting himself up to be worshipped in God's temple. As we've seen, it's hard to read Paul's words here in any way other than that by the time the satanic end-time dictator emerges, the temple will have been rebuilt in Jerusalem. (But not necessarily by the will of God, be it noted.) Right now, however, that temple does not exist; and if we believe that the 'next big event' we face will only happen after it's been rebuilt, it does become hard to feel the force of Jesus' challenge that He will come just when we don't expect (Matthew 24:42-44). Unless there is some time *after* the rapture when the temple can be rebuilt, we might well assume that Jesus will not come for us yet.[13]

A second example of this comes in Acts 3:19-21 which seems to say clearly (look at it for yourself!) that, before Jesus returns and God 'restores everything', there must be widespread repentance on the part of the Jews. (Presumably because in some way the ethnic Jewish nation has a vital part in the 'restoring of everything', as Paul makes clear in Romans 11 [see vv15,23,25].) We could have imagined that by refusing God's call here in Acts 3, the Jews shut themselves permanently out of God's plan for them to bring blessing to the nations (Acts 3:25). But Paul's whole argument in Romans 11 makes clear that that isn't so, and God still has a central, life-giving place in the plan for the ethnic Jews as they repent (eg 11:12-15). Again, however, this suggests that Christ's second coming as King to restore everything has certain major developments necessarily preceding it; and that too implies that it must be separate from a completely unexpected rapture happening somewhat earlier.

On reflection, however, this isn't a totally conclusive argument. Although Jesus taught His disciples that His coming would be at an unexpected time, they also knew that certain things must happen before the 'next big event' occurred: particularly the death of Peter (John 21:18), which obviously had to be before the rapture, otherwise he wouldn't have been on earth to die; and, much greater, the completion of their calling to preach the gospel to every nation before the End would come (Matthew 24:14). So even if they had been taught (by Jesus or Paul) to expect an 'unexpected' rapture, they knew that there were things that had to happen *before* it. There might be other such things, and these could include the rebuilding of the temple and the repentance of large numbers of ethnic Jews. Evidently what Jesus said about the unexpectedness of His coming for His people doesn't inevitably mean there has to be a period after His coming for these things to happen.

6. A more substantial argument perhaps: If there is no 'pre-trib' rapture, if what we believers are looking ahead to is a time of unparalleled evil on earth, then the mentality we would be left with seems almost inevitably very different from the buoyancy with which the early Church talks about the future. It's hard not to accept LaHaye's point[14] that, if the next event we are to look forward to is indeed the rapture when Christ comes to 'rescue us from the coming wrath' (1 Thessalonians 1:10) and 'take [us] to be with [him]' (John 14:3), then we see why Paul describes our outlook as our 'blessed hope' (Titus 2:13).[15] If, in contrast, what we see ahead of us is only a time of unparalleled horror 'unequalled from the beginning of the world until now … How dreadful it will be in those days for pregnant women and nursing mothers!' (Matthew 24:21,19) – 'blessed hope' will not be the obvious way to summarise what the future means for us. Something we may approach with grim determination and firm trust in

God's strengthening, yes; but while we can make up our minds to 'eagerly await' Christ's return (Philippians 3:20), we do so only as we look beyond the massive evil that will come first. And perhaps this is indeed the mentality we find celebrated in, say, Hebrews 10:32-39. But Christ's coming at the end of this evil time might not be the most obvious thing to hope for; might not the most obviously 'blessed hope' be that we and those we love should die and go to be with Christ before these days come? If, however, the rapture is the 'next big event', then 'blessed hope' makes complete sense as what should characterise our whole Christian attitude to the future. But how can that be if the rapture is 'post-trib', and the future before Christ's return for us is seriously intimidating?

7. Or put this another way: To summarise what the future holds for us as a 'blessed hope' does seem to express a very different set of expectations from those facing the believers who (we are told) will live through the time of unequalled distress in Matthew 24:17-22, or who will suffer martyrdom en masse as in Revelation 13:15. How does it make sense to describe *these* people as 'rescued from the coming wrath' in the way that God promises us (see 1 Thessalonians 1:10)? So, then, do we not need to think of two separate groups: we who will be kept from the hour of trial (Revelation 3:10, perhaps) and rescued from the coming wrath by the 'blessed hope' of the 'pre-trib' rapture, and some separate group living for God *after* the rapture as the 'hero generation'?

8. But then who might these godly people be who live in that horrific period after the rapture? Here in fact is another argument for seeing the rapture as taking out the

Church as we know it *before* the time of unequalled distress. There do seem to be biblical reasons to think that in the final drama of our era, the *global* Church is no longer the centre of the picture, and God's purposes on earth have centred again on the people of God among the ethnic Jews, in the way spoken of in Romans 11:11-29.

Our next chapter will explore more thoroughly just what Jesus meant by the 'times of the Gentiles' being a period that has an end (Luke 21:24), presumably ending when (Romans 11:25) the 'full number of the Gentiles' has come into God's people and, with that, Israel's 'hardening' ceases. But we should at least note here the way that Revelation 7:3-8 is careful to flag up 12,000 people from each of the twelve historic Jewish tribes as 'servants of our God' with some crucial (albeit mysterious) role in this final crisis period; the way Daniel 12:7 tells us that it is the 'breaking of the power' of Israel as a nation that triggers the final crisis; and also Jesus' very specific concern in Matthew 24:14-21 to forewarn those living in Judaea (v16; people who for whatever reason are keeping the Sabbath meticulously, v20) about events which aren't totally easy to interpret but again do seem to be part of the final 1,260-day crisis of history (vv14,21-22,29).[16] All this suggests that with the 'times of the Gentiles' over (Luke 21:24), the godly Jews are now, temporarily at least, at the epicentre of God's purposes. And that in turn might well imply that the Church as we currently know it has been lifted out of the picture beforehand, by the rapture, to begin her heavenly destiny.[17]

Well, it may be so. But enough of the arguments; let's catch the glory of what this implies. The belief that Jesus may come (the rapture may happen) at any time, breaking forcefully into whatever we are doing – 'Maybe Today!', to quote a poster from the Billy Graham Association's *Decision* magazine – is a very powerful motivation for radical holiness. If what we've just outlined is true, here is the point: none of us who are believers may be alive at home tomorrow night. And all that will matter then will be what we've invested in the kingdom; everything else will be gone. We will see what has lasted (Matthew 6:20; 1 Corinthians 3:12-15) and what was really significant among our fears, our priorities, our goals, our efforts, our concerns. Tonight Jesus may say, 'Enough!' – it's time for the climax of history; three and a half unmistakeable years to prove to humanity what centuries so far have failed to do; and *then* everything put right – everything bursting into joy and glory beyond our imagination. *Thank You, Lord!*

And if we're not sure we're Christians, it's not clever to get left behind for the days of the Animal, and left out of the glory. (Isn't that possibility something to tell people about?) We have no idea what heaven is like – we've never tasted infinite love and joy. But it wouldn't be clever to suddenly find out (just when we don't expect it) that we've missed out on all that really matters in existence.

'Maybe today'?!

Why disbelieve in a 'pre-trib' rapture?

What we've just said about the rapture doesn't command universal agreement, even among Christians who take the more 'literal' approach to what the Bible says about the future (let alone the more novel approach of Tom Wright[18]). Many Bible Christians are not convinced by this 'pre-trib' position (to quote the popular shorthand), that God snatches His people out before the final crisis. Instead, they see what we're told about the rapture as being illustrated by what citizens of that era would do to welcome a respected ruler – as he drew near they would go out of their city to meet him, and then come back with him, sharing the joy and glory of his arrival. So for the 'post-trib' position, the rapture of 1 Thessalonians 4 is not the 'next big thing', because it happens at (or almost at) the end of the 1,260-day crisis; we are caught up to meet the Lord in the air right when He returns to earth to reign.

There are three poor arguments for this 'post-trib' position for us to get out of the way before we turn to the significant ones.

1. All this about the rapture is *just too American*. That attitude's racist, and we should discount it; but that doesn't mean we don't sense it sometimes in the background to debates on this topic.

2. A gut feeling that all this stuff about planes and cars crashing just feels far too sensational, like B-movie science fiction. Well, so it may, but the end of history as we know it might well have a sensational feel! Ah, but wouldn't the 'leftovers' (as the Sky Atlantic series called them), the people 'left behind', be panicked into mass repentance if such dramatic things had happened? Possibly, but we know our own stubborn hearts; rather than admit we've been catastrophically foolish, we may well accept any possible alternative explanation. Indeed 2 Thessalonians 2:11 speaks of God allowing a 'powerful delusion' at this

time. (And no doubt the media would clamp down on any realisation of what had really happened, in the interests of keeping the peace.)

3. Belief in the rapture is sometimes seen as accompanying a selfish disinterest in the kinds of social, political and environmental engagement that are our biblical responsibility: because we may not be around in this world for long, there is no point in getting too involved in its affairs and needs. Perhaps there are some 'pre-trib' adherents who (probably from other motivations) think that way. But we can never dismiss a belief just because some of its adherents have drawn unwise and unnecessary conclusions from it. The fact that we are only temporarily in this world, and indeed may suddenly leave it, is not a reason for living anything but Christlike lives every second we are here. If as Christians we are renting a house only temporarily, that is not a justification for trashing the place. Global poverty and trade justice, climate change and care for the environment (the judgement of Revelation 11:18 is specifically stated as God 'destroying those who destroy the earth'), sex trafficking, internet pornography, the arms trade, sanctity of life: these issues and the others must be on our agenda simply because we are called to love our neighbours as ourselves, however long or short may be our residence here. Matthew 25 tells us that when the Son of Man comes in His kingdom, a big question will be, what did *you* do about the hungry, the immigrant, the sick, the imprisoned?

But now for five further arguments for the rapture being 'post-tribulation'. (As Paul says, 'I speak to sensible people; judge ... what I say'![19])

1. First an argument that is again not directly from Scripture, but it does carry weight for me. Christians holding the 'pre-trib' position have a clear sequence of events: rapture, then tribulation, then Christ's coming in glory, followed indeed by the millennium. I haven't forgotten sitting with my brother-in-law on the grass in a Berlin park where he pointed out tellingly that this sequence of events, so regularly (and, apparently, necessarily) set out in 'pre-trib' books and charts, simply doesn't appear in the Bible. That is true; and if the 'pre-trib' position is correct, it seems (to me at least) strikingly odd.

2. There's a related issue. The New Testament has many references to Christ's return: waiting 'for His Son from heaven' is one of the three key marks of those who have turned to God in 1 Thessalonians 1:10; 'we eagerly await a Saviour from there' (heaven), says Paul in Philippians 3:20; it is 'to those who are waiting for him' that Christ comes to bring salvation in Hebrews 9:28. And there are many others. But among all these, if the rapture really is the 'next event', definitely separate in time from Christ's open return, it's surprising that the New Testament is so little concerned to make this distinction clear. Again that might be because, just as the Old Testament's readers had not been shown how Christ's first coming was separated from the second, so it was only as the New Testament proceeded (and particularly after Paul received a special revelation about this? – see the ESV of 1 Thessalonians 4:15), that it became plain that the second coming itself had two phases. Making this clear had not been a priority, because both phases were so far away.

Nevertheless, there are really very few passages that can be pointed to with any conviction as making this distinction. There are the references to God not destining us to pass through the 'coming wrath' in 1 Thessalonians 1:10 and 5:9, which we looked at briefly in the previous section; and sometimes Revelation 3:10 is read this way too. And there is Matthew 24 and its parallel in Mark 13. But even these last are rather debatable.[20]

The really key verses here, as we noted in the previous section, are Matthew 24:36-44, particularly verses 40-41: 'Two men will be in the field; one will be taken and the other left. Two women will be grinding with a hand mill; one will be taken and the other left.' As we have seen, these can certainly be read (in the light of God's subsequent revelations) as referring to a rapture that 'takes' believers away to safety, just like Noah (v38), *before* the tribulation. And reading them that way does explain the very puzzling shift from v33, which clearly encourages Christ's followers living through the events of vv15-24 to sense the approach of the climax of history, to verse 42 and verse 44, emphasising that 'that day' will happen when people simply aren't expecting it – which might perhaps be a surprising thing to say if they were living through the horrific times described in Revelation.[21]

However, there is a problem in relating even these verses to a 'pre-trib' rapture, and it comes when we look carefully at the parallel teaching in Luke 17:26-35, apparently given on a different occasion but using very similar words. (Compare Luke 17:26-27 and 34-35 to Matthew 24:37-41.) According to Luke 17:30, these words in verses 26ff are describing 'the day when the Son of Man is *revealed*' (emphasis mine), which does seem an odd way to speak of the rapture *in distinction from* Christ's open, visible return. And then when we look at the context of the words 'Two women will be grinding grain together; one will be taken and the other left' in Luke 17:35, so very similar to Matthew 24:41, it might seem from Luke 17:31 to be more a warning of judgement coming on Judaea (whether that be in AD70 or at the End). (Indeed, a whole number of issues circle around this question: please see Appendix B for an attempt to explore and disentangle them.)

So, returning to Matthew 24, this still leaves us needing to explain the clear contrast between the unexpectedness of the coming in verses 36-44 and the strong encouragement in verse 33 to sense the imminence of the open coming of the Son of Man in the clouds in verses 27,30. But the Luke parallels must create some uncertainty as to whether even this last section of Matthew 24 is speaking of the rapture. And in that case, if the rapture is indeed an event separate in time from Christ's open return, it becomes even more surprising that the New Testament does so little to make this clear.

The interesting thing is that there is one more verse in Matthew 24 that makes complete sense as describing the rapture, namely verse 31: Christ 'will send his angels with a loud trumpet call, and they will gather his elect from the four winds, from one end of the heavens to the other'.[22] But here's the problem: if verse 31 is describing the rapture, the most natural way to read it (coming as it does after verses 21-30) is definitely at the *end* of the time of 'distress' in verse 21, so post-tribulation, and as an integral part of

Christ's open return described in the previous verse, verse 30. Again, of course, this could be because God was not yet revealing clearly that the second coming would be in two phases, and so verse 30 and verse 31 could be separated in time, just like Jesus' two comings in Isaiah 61:1-2 or Zechariah 9:9-13. Nevertheless, if verse 31 and verses 36-44 are both describing a 'pre-trib' rapture, we might have expected them to be together, rather than separated by verses 33-34 with their apparent focus on the events of the tribulation. We are left, then, with the fact that there is hardly anywhere in Scripture that can be pointed to with total conviction as distinguishing between the rapture and Christ's open return in glory.

3. In contrast, there are at least three key passages that can seem quite challenging for the 'pre-trib rapture' point of view. The first two are again in 2 Thessalonians.

Look at the NIV of 2 Thessalonians 1:6-8. Paul encourages the church there in Macedonia that God:

> will pay back trouble to those who trouble you and *give relief to you* who are troubled, and to us as well. *This will happen when the Lord Jesus is revealed* from heaven in blazing fire with his powerful angels. He will punish those who do not know God and do not obey the gospel of our Lord Jesus.
> *(Emphasis mine)*

Again we may choose to say that Paul is simply not that concerned about the distinction between the rapture and the second coming in glory. Otherwise, however, it might seem that this event of 'relief' from persecution for the

Christians (which must surely be the rapture) comes at the same time as Christ's being revealed 'in blazing fire with his powerful angels' to judge the hostile, unbelieving world – which is surely His open second coming.

4. Then there is the following chapter, 2 Thessalonians 2 again. At the start of this chapter Paul is carefully warning the Thessalonians against thinking that the 'day of the Lord', the crisis of history, has already begun. But his reassuring argument focuses on the fact that that day of crisis will not come 'until the rebellion occurs and the man of lawlessness is revealed' (v3). If the rapture indeed happens near the *start* of the 'day of the Lord', we might surely have expected him simply to say, 'Don't worry, you won't be around at that time of crisis because the rapture will have occurred.'[23] Well, possibly just that is the implication of verse 1, which could be translated 'By reason of' or 'On account of the coming of our Lord Jesus Christ' (Paul uses the same word here as in 1 Thessalonians 4:15-17 about the rapture) 'and our being gathered to him, we ask you, brothers, not to become easily unsettled'; and having said that, in verse 3 Paul adds a second reason for them not to be alarmed, that the day of the Lord won't come until the rise of evil has reached its zenith with the Animal deifying himself in the temple.[24] Or again, perhaps the reason is that the 'day' of which Paul speaks, that desperately difficult period of the 1,260 days, will begin, not with the rapture itself (which may be somewhat earlier), but with the revelation of the 'man of lawlessness', the Animal whose actions are its hallmark; and so Paul focuses on the fact that this hasn't happened and therefore the 'day' has not yet begun. Or yet again, perhaps their fear

– overreacting to his warning in 1 Thessalonians 5:2-3? – is that somehow the rapture has already occurred and they've missed it;[25] and therefore Paul points them to other reasons why they shouldn't think that the 'day of the Lord has already come'.

5. The other challenging passage is 1 Corinthians 15:51-52, where we learn that the time when we believers will be transformed into our spiritual bodies – presumably the rapture – is at the '*last* trumpet' (emphasis mine). This verse fits very well with the angels gathering the elect with a 'loud trumpet call' in Matthew 24:31, which as we've seen is most naturally (though not unavoidably) read as happening at the time of Christ's open appearing of 24:30, and *after* the tribulation of 24:15-28. But the challenging question about the Corinthians passage is how the 'last trumpet' of the rapture can come at any point but the end of the sequence of trumpets Revelation depicts occurring throughout the tribulation; and in Revelation the last trumpet (11:15) seems to come at the close of the terrible period of forty-two months or 1,260 days (11:2-3).[26] Again, however, the argument is powerful but not totally conclusive: it is possible to argue that (whatever reality is described by the trumpet of Matthew 24 and 1 Corinthians 15) it is the 'last' *of its historical kind;* whereas Revelation's trumpets, like the vials, are somewhat more symbolic in significance, being used to structure the book's narrative.

So there's the data. What do you think?

So what?

So there are two scenarios. It's very possible that the final crisis is near. If so, what is the 'next big event'? It's hard to say[27] – and *maybe God meant it like that*!

For me personally, either position is possible. We don't know. And I wonder if God has left it deliberately unclear because we benefit practically from both possibilities. It's vital to live aware that Christ may come at any minute to take us home. It's also vital to live aware that being Christians may involve us in facing serious persecution; it's happening in many other countries, and may happen one day in ours, whether it's the end times or not. (What could prove disastrous is the unpreparedness for both that comes from ignoring all the Bible passages embodying what the Lord has told us about all this.)

Economic breakdown in 1920s Germany led rapidly to the rise of the dictatorship of Hitler, and it's all too easy to see how economic or environmental breakdown could have such results again – with the warning from Revelation that the final 'firm government' will turn out to be demonic. As we've said, maybe we or our children will be the 'hero generation' called to stay faithful to Christ when the Animal comes, who will refuse the Animal's mark (whatever that turns out to be), even if it costs us our lives. But even if we believe the rapture will save us from the worst time, there is a chance we may face the early days of the Animal's reign, or our own country may anyway start treating believers as badly as others have done. Either way, we should make it a goal to get used to pressure, seeing it as training.

What matters in that case is developing a faith that's robust, not childish and dependent on our feelings and external circumstances; cultivating solid roots in the Word, and the habit of living it out whatever the cost; because we know that the gospel really is true and is the only way to heaven and the infinite joy and glory of God. 'He who stands firm to the end will be saved,' said Jesus (Matthew 24 again, this time v13). We will need supernatural grace and power: God has promised it in (not before!) the time of need (Hebrews 4:16); and He guarantees that He 'will not let you be tempted beyond what you can bear' (1 Corinthians 10:13). But He also tells us to 'arm yourselves' with Christ's attitude (1 Peter 4:1), to 'put on the full armour of God' (piece by piece) for 'when the day of evil comes' (Ephesians 6:13). (That's worth doing also because these 'days of evil' can come in everyday life!)

In other words: *Just maybe the 'post-tribbers' should be listened to. If so, I will need supernatural power; God has promised it. But if so, Lord, how should I pray, how should I aim to grow? Help me look the issue in the face!*

Or maybe the 'pre-tribbers' are right! Maybe what comes next really is the rapture and 1 Thessalonians 4:17: Jesus suddenly takes His people home. It's vital for us to live conscious that this might happen at any minute. Jesus said that when He comes back, it will be exactly when we aren't expecting it (Matthew 24:36-44). We must be prepared – as He said, 'Be always on the watch … like men waiting for their master to return' (Luke 21:36; 12:36). We should live our whole lives ready for Him to come.

This possible scenario is a powerful motivator for evangelism. It would be catastrophic for anyone we care about to get left behind, suddenly left out, too late; and we know that God's offer of salvation does have a deadline (2 Corinthians 6:1-2). If you're not a Christian, think: in this case Jesus is saying that before you close this book, history as we know it may end; the die could be cast, and we could be left behind to face the final crisis of history. Maybe that focuses your mind, as it does mine. If we don't know we're forgiven, if we don't know we're Jesus' son or daughter, now is the only time we possess to sort that out. 'You must also be ready, because the Son of Man will come at an hour when you do not expect him' is the counsel from Jesus' own mouth!

And if we are Jesus-followers: we live on the edge of eternity. It's always been so: any day may see our lives end in a car crash. Or Christ may return: maybe today. Either way, later today we may see Him face to face. Our 'Bridegroom' will come, utterly unexpectedly; we'll give account to our loving Lord of the lives and the years He's entrusted to us (Romans 14:12). And then come millions of years of glory and joy beyond our imagination! But to grasp that Christ may really be 'standing at the door' (James 5:9) is to grasp that radical holiness matters. It matters that we do those things that last for eternity, so what are they? They do include our secular work (Colossians 3:17,23), and the social, political and environmental engagement that comes from loving our neighbours as ourselves!

'Are you ready for the day of the Lord?' asked Bob Dylan on his *Saved* album.[28] How would I live if I knew

Christ would return this month? What would matter more? What wouldn't? Because He may!

So, loving God, help me to live for You! Give me supernatural strength when I need it. I could not do alone what we've talked about here, but only by Your grace. But that's always how it is. Help me learn to build steel into my soul from Your Word. Help me learn to feed on Your grace, through Your Word. Help me learn how to be an 'overcomer', as Revelation says. Help me grasp the fact that You may come back at any time; and in the light of that, to live for radical holiness, and to do those things that last forever! Amen!

Notes

[1] F F Bruce's commentary says that 'caught up' in 1 Thessalonians 4:17 implies 'violent action'; *1 & 2 Thessalonians* (Word, 1982), p102. The parallel usages in Acts 8:39, Acts 23:10 and 2 Corinthians 12:2,3 are very illuminating.

[2] I have to say that, for me, the implausibility of the alternatives as to who or what this 'restrainer' that is 'taken out of the way' might be (the preaching of the gospel and the law and order embodied in the Roman empire seem the two most popular suggestions) is a strong argument for the whole 'rapture' framework.

[3] Should we see this as a brief reversal of Pentecost, a return to the pre-Pentecost situation, before the Holy Spirit is poured out on all flesh more fully than ever once Christ returns as King?

[4] Bruce (p102) notes that the word used for 'meet' in 1 Thessalonians 4:17 can imply coming back with a dignitary – see Matthew 25:6 and Acts 28:15. One can see why this classical custom would fit well with God's desire to honour His persecuted people, 2 Thessalonians 1:10, Colossians 3:4.

[5] As one of the vast numbers of people who were blessed because of the Jesus Movement, it grieves me a bit that the story of its successes and failures is almost forgotten now. It is, after all, the only time we've come close to seizing the high ground of contemporary youth culture in the last hundred years. See for example R M Enroth, E E Ericson and C B Peters, *The Story of the Jesus People* (Paternoster, 1972).

[6] There are several versions of this powerful song on YouTube, including the one used in *The Leftovers* television series and another by DC Talk.

[7] We don't have space to look at this here, but that would be particularly so if, as Daniel 9:27 seems to be saying, the

beginning of that final terrible three and a half years is marked by the Animal breaking a treaty with Israel and forcibly desecrating its temple – the event also highlighted as a sign by Jesus in Matthew 24:15. See also Daniel 12:7.

[8] It's true that the 'normality' of verse 38 could refer to the people of the world generally, and could easily be happening even when believers specifically are facing terrible persecution. On the other hand, it does seem very strange as a description even of unbelievers living through the end-time horrors described in Revelation.

[9] There may be other ways of resolving this first enigma, but they are not straightforward. Douglas Moo (in *Three Views on the Rapture* , ed Gleason Archer [Zondervan, 1996], p253), cites E E Ellis to the effect that 'Evidence from Qumran indicates that "generation" could be used to indicate the last generation before the end'. Moo suggests that the apparently blatant clash can be resolved in that the uncertainty of verse 36 applies to Jesus' time (effectively 'No one knows now') and to 'every generation except the last'; whereas the certainty of verse 33 applies to 'this generation' (v34), whom His hearers would easily understand as the last generation, the one that sees the 'fig-tree' signs, and for whom verses 32-35 apply. When *they* see these signs, they will know that, despite the terrible things that are happening, the Lord is 'at the door' and they won't all die before the Lord returns in glory. However, that would have been a strangely misleading message for Jesus to leave for the generation that lived through AD70; surely then, when they saw the abomination in the temple, they would have seen themselves as this special 'last generation', the one that would know they were about to see the End and His imminent return. And isn't that precisely the disastrous error Jesus was seeking to guard them against in verse 6? Equally, the problem disappears if most of the time up to Matthew 24:34 Jesus is speaking of AD70, and He moves on to speak of His second

coming only from verse 35 on. But see Appendix A for a discussion of the major problems in that theory.

10 Paul had been teaching them carefully about the end-time 'day of the Lord' and the satanic dictator central to it (2 Thessalonians 2:5). Why had it been so much on his mind? Perhaps because (knowing the second coming might possibly be soon) he was watching developments in imperial Rome with considerable unease?

11 In contrast, Moo, p186, paraphrases Paul's argument as being that their salvation (vv5,9) 'should act as a stimulus to holy living – holy living that will enable them to avoid experiencing the Day [ie "wrath"] in its unexpected and destructive features'; but that seems a little odd – holy living won't keep them from being 'destructively' slaughtered, Revelation 13:15.

12 Certainly Revelation 14:14-20 seems to take us to the End. On first reading these verses might seem to be entirely about judgement (particularly in the light of the similar words in Joel 3:13). Earlier in the chapter, however, we've heard of people who are the 'firstfruits to God' (v4), and if 'firstfruits' is positive in verse 4, the full harvest in verse 16 could well be positive too, with Christ's Church being the 'positive' harvest of the earth, the fruit of its history (cf Matthew 13:23; John 12:24). So in that case Revelation 14:14-16 and 14:19-20 give the two sides of the final reaping, to blessing (in the rapture) and to judgement, just like in Matthew 13:28-30 and 37-43. Compare also Matthew 24:30-31.

13 There isn't a problem with the length of time available after the rapture for these things to happen. Assuming that the rapture happens near the start of the final crisis (rather than towards its end, as 'post-tribbers' would argue), there is no passage – at least that I can see – that would narrow down how close the two may be. Indeed, there is scholarly debate in the USA between those who see the rapture as occurring close to

the start of the 1,260 days and others who (drawing on the end of the prophecy in Daniel 9, which we don't have space to consider here) expect it an extra three and a half years before that.

[14] In Tim LaHaye, *The Rapture* (Harvest House, 2002), pp69-70.

[15] Whereas, in contrast, the Old Testament does warn ethnic Israel of a very tough time to come before the era of great blessing: eg in Zechariah 14 or Jeremiah 30.

[16] We should note, too, that the teaching of Matthew 24 about Jesus' coming flows on specifically from His words in 23:38-39. Here, the 'you' who 'will not see me again until you say, "Blessed is he who comes in the name of the Lord",' refers undeniably to ethnic Israel and their relations to their rejected Messiah. Arguably this is the context for Matthew 24.

[17] This links to a final reason why those of us who believe in a literal golden age or millennium after Christ's return – and for good reasons, as we'll see in chapter 5 – should also believe in a 'pre-trib' rapture. Who are the people who live through the final crisis into the millennium and then have children there (eg Isaiah 65:20,23)? How can it be those who have participated in the rapture, when 'with the trumpet call of God' (1 Thessalonians 4:16), 'at the last trumpet', their bodies have been transformed and transfigured (1 Corinthians 15:52)? Given what Jesus says in Matthew 22:30, is it likely that they will then have children? So again, does there not need to be another group of people such as we have been discussing, who will enter the millennium, totally separate from those who will be taken in the rapture? But this argument isn't quite as conclusive as, for example, LaHaye thinks (*The Rapture*, p130), because of the mass repentance of ethnic Jews we considered above in #5. It would seem from Zechariah 12:10 that this repentance occurs only when Christ visibly reappears; the greatest number of these repentant Jews, then, may not have been involved even if

there were a 'post-trib' rapture of Christians, and therefore may be the ones who survive to populate the millennium. Nor can we be sure who Jesus is talking about in Matthew 25:34 and whether they are entering the millennium. That an 'iron sceptre' will be exercised in 'authority over the nations' both by Christ (Revelation 12:5) and the overcomers (Revelation 2:26-27) might imply that Wayne Grudem could be right in suggesting that at Christ's return many unbelievers 'will simply surrender without trusting Christ and will thus enter the millennium as unbelievers' (*Bible Doctrine* [Inter-Varsity Press, 2009], p450). Or (to my mind, more plausibly) we may also be looking at the children of those unbelievers, who were themselves not judged along with their parents when Christ returned, and so entered the glorious millennium.

[18] Indeed, some readers may be amazed that the idea of a 'pre-trib' rapture can even be considered after Tom Wright's diatribe against it in his popular *Surprised by Hope* (SPCK, 2007). And here is where I wish this were an academic book with space to analyse Wright's deep dislike of 'rapture theology'. It isn't, so I can only note that Wright builds on several assumptions which, listed together, make a somewhat outlandish package. Wright argues (1) that Jesus' own beliefs and concerns are, first and foremost, those of a first-century Jew (see also *Jesus and the Restoration of Israel*, ed Carey Newman [Paternoster, 1999], pp260,270); and because the prime concerns of the mainstream of first-century Jewry were 'political' ones, the relationship of Israel to their Roman conquerors and how God might step in soon to end Israel's exile and place her in a position of glory, these, not the overall future, must be seen as the questions at the heart of Jesus' teaching too. (This although God's input normally seems to be designed to help His people have very different concerns from their cultural mainstream.) (2) That therefore the gospel passages we usually read as about the second coming are all really about Jesus' first coming, and then

God's coming in judgement on Israel through Rome in AD70. (3) That, in fact, 'during his earthly ministry, Jesus said nothing about his return' (*Surprised by Hope*, p137) (Matthew 16:27? Matthew 19:28? Matthew 23:39? Matthew 24:30?? Mark 14:62?? John 14:3??) – although the early Church did (but again, what started them doing so if not Jesus' own teaching?) (4) That the passages about Jesus coming on the clouds are all about His coming to the Father (Daniel 7:13), not His coming back to earth (but again, Matthew 24:30? Mark 14:62 [note the order]? Revelation 1:7?) (5) That Jesus will certainly not 'descend like a spaceman from the sky' (*Surprised by Hope*, p147; on p140 Wright quotes Acts 1:9-11 yet ignores the fact that it says Jesus 'will come back in the same way you have seen him go into heaven'. In *Jesus and the Restoration of Israel*, p271, he describes [or sets aside?] this crucial chapter, with no evidence, as a 'stylized narrative'); however, Wright gives no description of how Christ's return will happen instead of a 'spaceman descent'. (6) That 1 Thessalonians 4 on the second coming is '*not* to be taken as a literal description of what Paul thinks will happen' – but he offers no proof; remarkably, he sees the reference to Christ's descent from heaven as an allusion to Moses descending Sinai, which isn't mentioned in the passage at all, rather than to the promise of Acts 1:11 which would have been so important to these early lovers of Jesus (*Surprised by Hope*, pp143-44). It's also quite hard to feel that Wright has listened seriously to any intelligent proponent of the position he attacks. If he had, he would surely have learned that most proponents of the rapture believe in a millennium to come in which this present world is transformed in glorious ways, and most certainly not that 'God intends to destroy the present space-time universe … quite soon now' (*Surprised by Hope*, p103).

[19] 1 Corinthians 10:15.

[20] Ironically, because many American 'pre-trib' writers are

dispensationalists concerned to argue that Matthew 24 is written entirely for Israel rather than for the Church, they do not see the rapture in these verses either; see, for example, Charles Feinberg, *Millennialism* (Moody Press, 1980), pp231,298, and LaHaye, *The Rapture*, p204. But this just makes the absence of biblical passages distinguishing the rapture from Christ's appearing in glory even more glaringly obvious.

[21] It's an even more surprising thing to say if, as Tom Wright argues, these verses (indeed the entire chapter) refer primarily to AD70. Either the Roman invasion of AD70 would be all too obviously imminent (see vv32-33), or it will come as a complete surprise (vv37-39), including to the disciples (vv42,44); it can't be both.

[22] We might be a little surprised by the reference here to angels; but there are other situations where angels are presented as the immediate agents of something that elsewhere the Lord Himself is described as doing; eg Exodus 23:23, Numbers 20:16 or Galatians 3:19. However, William Kelly, who is 'pre-trib', sees this verse instead as part of the Jewish focus of the chapter, referring to the angels gathering the Jews who have been scattered throughout the nations (*Lectures on the Second Coming of the Lord Jesus Christ* [A S Rouse, n.d.], p213). There is undeniably a fair amount about that in the Old Testament – see Deuteronomy 30:3-5 and Isaiah 11:11-12; 14:2; 43:5-6; 66:20; Ezekiel 39:25-28. But it's the nations who bring the remaining Jews back to Palestine, not angels, Isaiah 14:2; 66:20.

[23] A point well-argued by John Piper in http://www.desiringgod.org/sermons/what-must-happen-before-the-day-of-the-lord (accessed 19th February 2018). Interestingly, Piper describes himself as a post-tribulationist and 'hope-filled premillennialist', a combination which would be (sadly?) unusual on this side of the Atlantic in anyone subscribing to Piper's kind of Reformed theology. See also

https://www.desiringgod.org/articles/are-you-becoming-a-post-millennialist (accessed 28th March 2018). Moo comments (p189) that if the Thessalonians had been taught a pre-trib rapture, one might have expected them to conclude this themselves. But then again, 1 Thessalonians 4:15 may seem to present some at least of what Paul says about the rapture as being a new revelation ('This we declare to you by a word from the Lord', ESV) which came after his departure and significantly expanded the teaching he had given when he had been with them (2 Thessalonians 2:5).

[24] Some writers point out that the word the NIV and ESV translate as 'rebellion' in verse 3 – 'that day will not come until the rebellion occurs' – can be translated 'departure', and argue that this refers to the rapture; but that is not widely accepted.

[25] One objection to this idea is that then the false teachers might seem to have missed the rapture too. But the 'letter supposed to have come from Paul' could have been an earlier threat that the rapture was imminent and that if they didn't listen to the false teachers in Thessalonica, their entire church would be left behind; and the false teachers were presumably now saying that, because the rest of the church didn't listen to them, that has happened.

[26] Indeed, many commentators read the 'two witnesses' of that chapter, Revelation 11, as a symbolic portrayal of all God's people on earth at that time, and hence can see 11:12 as the (post-tribulation) rapture.

[27] For a more in-depth debate, see *Three Views on the Rapture*, ed Gleason Archer. But let the buyer beware: the 'post-trib' essay by Douglas Moo is by far the most compelling.

[28] From 'Are You Ready?', copyright © 1980 by Special Rider Music. All rights reserved. International copyright secured. Reprinted by permission.

Chapter Four

So How Does Ethnic Israel Fit Into All This?

'I will create Jerusalem to be a delight
and its people a joy.
I will rejoice over Jerusalem
and take delight in my people ...
Never again will there be in it
an infant who lives but a few days,
or an old man who does not live out his years;
he who dies at a hundred will be thought a mere youth ...
Before they call I will answer;
while they are still speaking I will hear.
The wolf and the lamb will feed together,
and the lion will eat straw like the ox,
but dust will be the serpent's food.
They will neither harm nor destroy
on all my holy mountain,'
says the LORD.
(Isaiah 65:18-20,24-25)

Jesus returns. And then the world is transformed. A glorious new age, a golden age, begins. What will it be like? (And: What's all that about a wonderful 'millennium' to come?)

We'll dig into these questions in the next chapter. But to know how to handle them at all, we need to explore first what God says about something else: *Is there a 'Jewishness', a Jerusalem-centredness, about the end of history?*

What follows may be the most intense chapter in this book. But the answer to this question can lead to whole swathes of the Bible coming alive for us, so let's persevere!

We've already seen, in the preceding chapter, how this issue – is there a key place in God's end-time purposes for ethnic Israel? and for the land of Israel in particular? – has implications for whether as the global Church we expect to be delivered before all hell breaks loose here, or whether it seems to be our calling to face the final crisis and the Animal. But it's a key issue much more broadly, between the more 'literal' and the more 'non-literal' approaches to the future; and it's particularly significant now as we ask, what happens after Jesus returns as King? Is that the end of the planet, or (before He brings in a completely 'new heaven and new earth' [Revelation 21:1]) does God have a glorious plan for *this* earth restored – a purpose in which the Jews are somehow very significant, and where the restored earth is somehow centred on a literal Jerusalem?

But the question is also: What did Jesus mean when He prophesied the fall of Jerusalem in Luke 21:24, by speaking of the 'times of the Gentiles' as a period that would start then but clearly have an end? *What happens after the 'times of the Gentiles' are over?* And what about when Paul looks ahead to a time when (Romans 11:25) the 'full number of the Gentiles' have joined God's people, at which point ethnic Israel's 'hardening' comes to an end and they are used by God to bring 'life from the dead' (Romans 11:15), because ultimately 'God's gifts and his call' to them are 'irrevocable' (v29)? What does all this tell us about what happens in the time of the End?

Goodbye ethnic Israel?

We are now in another area where – it seems to me – a more 'literal' approach to future prophecy makes fascinating sense of many passages that can otherwise seem obscure and therefore be neglected. But not all Bible Christians see it this way. Let me try to summarise the debate.

My impression is that for the majority of British evangelical academics, ethnic Israel, and the land of Israel especially, have no further special part in God's purposes. And so the Old Testament promises to Israel are often applied *exclusively* to Christ and the Church (including, of course, its Jewish members). To quote J A Thompson in the Tyndale commentary on Deuteronomy:

> It is important for the Christian to realize that in the New Testament the Christian church (Gk. *ekklesia*) is regarded as the true people of God (James 1:1, 1 Peter 2:5,9,10). Christians are the true 'Jews' (Rom 2:29; cf Rev 2:9), Israel (Rom 9:6), Israel after the Spirit (Rom 8:1-11), the seed of Abraham (Gal 3:7,29), the Israel of God (Gal 6:16), the circumcision (Phil 3:3; Col 2:11), the peculiar [or, chosen] people (Titus 2:14; 1 Peter 2:9f; cf Ex

19:5) … [Paul] sees only one Israel into which the Gentiles are grafted [Thompson is referring here to Romans 11:17-24], so that there is no difference between the church and Israel. The true Israel was constituted through a faith relationship and not merely on the basis of physical descent.[1]

A fair amount of that is unarguable. And he could have strengthened his case further: first by noting how Galatians 3:16 explains that the promises 'spoken to Abraham and to his seed', for example about the land of Israel, were in fact spoken not to '"seeds", meaning many people, but "and to your seed", meaning one person, who is Christ' – and then, presumably, to anyone of any ethnic background who has come 'into Christ'. We inherit the promises to Abraham. (And in Romans 4:13 Paul summarises those promises to the effect that Abraham would be 'heir of the *world*' [emphasis mine], not just the land, and says they are for all believers whether Jews or Gentiles [4:16].)

Second, although the Old Testament contains many promises to the Jews, God made it clear that His promises often had a *conditional* element. God warns Israel in Jeremiah 18:

Like clay in the hand of the potter, so are you in my hand, O house of Israel … [If] I announce that a nation or kingdom is to be built up and planted, and if it does evil in my sight and does not obey me, then I will reconsider the good I had intended to do for it.

(The same principle is set out clearly in Deuteronomy 28:68, 1 Samuel 2:30 and 2 Chronicles 7:16-21.)

Third, Jesus explicitly warned the Jews of exactly this, that by rejecting Him they were putting themselves outside God's purposes of blessing: 'The kingdom of God will be taken away from you and given to a people who will produce its fruit,' He says in Matthew 21:43; and by the time of Acts 28:25-28 just this seems to be happening. 'In a word', then, says Motyer in *The Bible Speaks Today* commentary on James:

> 'Israel' is the name of the people of Jesus; it is the true and inalienable title of his church … [Jesus] was leading the Israel of the Old Covenant into its full, intended reality as the Israel of the New Covenant … Those who have put their faith in Jesus for salvation are Abraham's children and the Israel of God.[2]

As I say, a good deal of this is unarguable. But there are two huge 'howevers'.

First, the reinterpretation into (massively glorious!) spiritual terms of God's promises to Abraham, in Galatians 3 and Romans 4, says nothing about whether they have a double fulfilment. (Bible prophecies sometimes do: think for example of how the messianic psalms can be about David or Solomon and also about the Christ to come; or look at Matthew 2:15, or Isaiah 61:2, or 2 Samuel 7:12-14, or Zechariah 6:12.) The most important fulfilment, obviously, is the eternal one, the 'promise of the Spirit' (Galatians 3:14), and also that we – Jews and Gentiles together – are 'heirs of the world' (Romans 4:13,16). *But* this does not rule out a second fulfilment, centred concretely on the land of Israel, for Jesus' disciples in ethnic Israel. (A classic expression of this is Zechariah 2, which states unambiguously how 'Many nations will be joined with the LORD in that day and will become my people' [v11], but then adds equally clearly in the following verse, 'The LORD will inherit Judah as his portion *in the holy land* [emphasis mine] and will again choose Jerusalem.')

Second, there are limits to how far God's central promises are conditional upon what we humans do. *(Thank God for that!)* The last part of Ezekiel (see for example 37:22) prophesies the restoration of ethnic Israel (including even Ephraim, the disastrous northern half, which had vanished into obscurity by then), at a time of Jerusalem's complete failure and devastation. Isaiah 11:12-16 prophesies the regathering of both Israel and Judah 'from the four quarters of the earth' – but this promise appears precisely in the context of serious sin and failure, not just of the northern kingdom, Israel (allied treacherously, even as Isaiah was writing, with Syria against Judah), but also of Judah itself; and exactly at the time when God's purposes were shifting from the Jewish nation as a whole to the righteous remnant (chapters 7 and 8). God still has plans for the northern kingdom, even when its sinfulness is on the verge of bringing it to complete extinction. Indeed, for those of us who believe that the last half of Isaiah predates Jerusalem's fall, all the wonderful depictions of God's blessing to Jerusalem in these chapters come when it was already clear that Judah's sin was so serious that exile was inevitable (39:6). It was at such a time that God gave the most spectacular revelations of its glorious future. When it comes to God's central purposes for the world, whatever people do, His declared intentions stand firm. *(Thank You, Lord!)*

So is there evidence in the New Testament of anything so irrevocable in God's end-time purposes for ethnic Israel?

Romans 9-11 seem to make clear that the answer is Yes. (Please read 11:11-29 at least!) Here Paul states that God does have such a future purpose, and indeed that ethnic Israel's repentance, coming after 'the full number of the Gentiles has come in'(v25), will be followed by something dramatic enough to be described as 'life from the dead' (v15).[3] The jumping-off point of these chapters is the wonderful promise in 8:38-39: Nothing in the present, and nothing in the future, can separate us from the love of Christ! Ah – but what if that is only conditional? What can Paul have to say about God's promises to ethnic Israel (9:3), which now seems to have forfeited its place in God's love? What price God's promises to them?

In 9:6 Paul sets out his response to this: 'It is not as though God's word had failed'! And he then provides a several-sided answer as to how Israel still shares in the purposes of God. First, indeed, he does make the point that now 'Israel' is a complex entity; not everyone who is descended from Israel is Israel in the sense that counts (9:6 again). And then – having explained how Israel has got itself into trouble by its rebelliousness (10:21) – he makes clear that there is still a remnant of ethnic Israel that is yet in the plan (11:1-5). What is crucial for our purposes, however, is what he goes on to say next: God has not rejected His ancient chosen people, and the time will come when ethnic Israel will be brought back into the plan

(11:11-15, 25-27). And that, exults Paul, will produce colossal regeneration, nothing less than 'life from the dead' (v15). In the culmination ethnic Israel still has a place. God is faithful and His promises are not unreliable: in fact when it comes to something as central to history as God's overall plan with His chosen people – here is the verse that counts – *'God's gifts and his call are irrevocable'*(v29, emphasis mine)!

Old Testament Israel and the future

That seems clear enough. But if we really want the facts, the full, glorious picture, we need to be serious about grasping God's Old Testament revelation and drinking in the sheer volume of glorious, joyous promises in its less well-known books about ethnic Israel and, often, its land. Again, I personally find the 'non-literal' interpretation of all this implausible because it simply doesn't handle enough of the data.[4]

Where do we begin? Perhaps in the strange thirtieth chapter of Deuteronomy, prefaced as it is with the enigmatic comment that 'the secret things belong to the LORD our God' (29:29).[5] It is difficult to see Deuteronomy 30:3-4 speaking of Israel being banished to 'all the nations where [God] scattered you ... the most distant land under the heavens', as foretelling the exile in Babylon; surely this sounds much more like the global dispersion of the Jews after AD70. But then when were the next verses fulfilled, verses 5-6?

> He will bring you to the land that belonged to your fathers ... He will make you more prosperous and numerous than your fathers. The

LORD your God will circumcise your hearts and
the hearts of your descendants, so that you may
love him with all your heart and with all your
soul, and live.

This also didn't really get fulfilled in the return after the
exile; are we not looking therefore at an end-time national
repentance and blessing?

Similar questions arise with the predictions in Isaiah
14:2 (where Alec Motyer, who does not support the overall
approach we are setting out here, remarks in his superb
Tyndale commentary on Isaiah that:

> What actually happened at the return from
> Babylon (539BC) in no way fulfilled this ... There
> was [then] no international acclaim or will to
> help, no reversal of the captor-captive roles[6]

whereas Isaiah says, `Nations will take [Israel] and bring
them to their own place ... They will make captives of their
captors and rule over their oppressors'); Isaiah 43:5 ('I will
bring your children from the east, and gather you from the
west'); Zechariah 10:9-10 ('Though I scatter them among
the peoples, yet in distant lands they will remember me.
They and their children will survive, and they will return.
I will bring them back'); and Ezekiel 39:21-29, where,
strikingly, verse 22 ('From that day forward' – that is, from
the time of God's destruction of the mighty forces invading
Palestine – 'the house of Israel will know that I am the
LORD their God') shows that Israel had been brought back
to its land in unbelief – and yet God's promises still held
firm. It is hard not to see in these passages, first the

dramatic events of 1948 when Israel came back into existence as a nation in Palestine after a gap of nearly nineteen centuries, just as literally minded Bible Christians had long been expecting them to do; and then pointers towards something still greater in store for Israel in the days to come.

There's much more in Isaiah, particularly about the glory to be centred on Israel in the future – verses often not at all easy to reapply to the Church. Consider just four examples:

> Foreigners will rebuild your walls, and their kings will serve you. Though in anger I struck you, in favour I will show you compassion. Your gates will always stand open, they will never be shut, day or night, so that men may bring you the wealth of the nations – their kings led in triumphal procession. For the nation or kingdom that will not serve you will perish; it will be utterly ruined … The sons of your oppressors will come bowing before you.
> *Isaiah 60:10-12,14*

> 'And they will bring all your [people], from all the nations, to my holy mountain in Jerusalem as an offering to the LORD – on horses, in chariots and wagons, and on mules and camels,' says the LORD. 'They will bring them, as the Israelites bring their grain offerings, to the temple of the LORD in ceremonially clean vessels.'
> *Isaiah 66:20*

Many peoples will come and say,
'Come, let us go up to the mountain of the LORD,
to the house of the God of Jacob.
He will teach us his ways,
so that we may walk in his paths.'
The law will go out from Zion,
the word of the LORD from Jerusalem.
He will judge between the nations
and will settle disputes for many peoples.
Isaiah 2:3-4

You will be called the City of Righteousness.
Isaiah 1:26

(Compare also Micah 4:2-8 and 7:11-20.)

(I have to admit that for me it's difficult to think of God making these promises to ethnic Israel and then saying, 'Well, in fact most of your own descendants won't benefit from what I promised, but that's all right because the people who will benefit will be called the new Israel; they will take over your name!' 'I will make an everlasting covenant with you, my faithful love promised to David', says God in the celebration of His unimaginable restoration in Isaiah 55:3; but in what sense does this promise have value for its recipients, if in the end Jewish identity is irrelevant and the blessing is passed to a [mostly] completely different group of God-fearers?)

Then there's Daniel. As God reveals the future in this book, ethnic Israel and its land seem central. Daniel 9:24-27 presents an amazing account of the sweep of history ordained by God 'to finish transgression, to put an end to sin, to atone for wickedness, to bring in everlasting righteousness, to seal up vision and prophecy and to anoint the Most Holy'. Astonishingly, we seem to be given here, far ahead and accurately, the timing of just when 'the Anointed One' (which is what 'Christ' means) will come (vv25-26), before he is 'cut off'. (Tom Wright notes that among first-century Jews there was great interest in calculating when Daniel's 'seventy weeks of years' might be completed, which many saw as happening in their own [and Jesus'] time.[7] He also cites Josephus' remarkable reference to this passage [in *Jewish Wars* 6:312-15], where Josephus 'spoke of an oracle in the Jewish Scriptures which predicted that, at that time, a world ruler would arise from Judea'.[8])

The important thing for us here is that this panorama of salvation history is summarised for Daniel as being 'decreed for your people *and* [which should remove any doubts about whether ethnic Israel is intended] *your holy city*' (emphasis mine). The panorama concludes[9] (v27) with someone unpleasant (presumably 'the ruler who will come' of v26) breaking his word (to Israel?) three and a half years before it all ends, and setting up an 'abomination that causes desolation' in the temple in Jerusalem – precisely what Jesus (in Matthew 24:15, 'spoken of through the prophet Daniel') and Paul (2 Thessalonians 2:4) highlighted as the key marker of the final crisis. Similarly, in Daniel 12:7 we learn that the final three and a half years head for completion 'when the power of the holy people has been finally broken', which sounds like the same national catastrophe (and again surely cannot refer to the Church).[10] So in Daniel too the people of Israel and its city seem central to the final drama.

Then there's Jeremiah. Jeremiah 3:16-18 hasn't happened to this day:

> 'In those days, when your numbers have increased greatly in the land,' declares the LORD, '[people] will no longer say, "The ark of the covenant of the LORD." It will never enter their minds or be remembered; it will not be missed, nor will another one be made. At that time they will call Jerusalem The Throne of the LORD, and all nations will gather in Jerusalem to honour the name of the LORD ... In those days the house of Judah will join the house of Israel, and together they will come from a northern land to the land I gave your forefathers as an inheritance.'

The prophecies concerning the restoration of Israel in Jeremiah 33 also remain unfulfilled (look at the wordings of verse 9 and verse 16 – and verse 18 is particularly interesting in declaring that the Levitical priests will never 'fail to have a man to stand before me continually to offer burnt offerings, to burn grain offerings and to present sacrifices', which appears, like the final chapters of Ezekiel, to speak of an end-time temple in Jerusalem). Verses 25-26 make the central point about ethnic Israel unmistakably clear for us:

> This is what the LORD says: 'If I have not established my covenant with day and night and the fixed laws of heaven and earth, then I will reject the descendants of Jacob and David my servant and will not choose one of his sons to rule over the descendants of Abraham, Isaac and

Jacob. For I will restore their fortunes and have compassion on them.'

Jeremiah 31:36-37 says the same, and makes clear too that these promises are not in the end conditional:

'Only if these decrees vanish from my sight,' declares the LORD,
'will the descendants of Israel ever cease to be a nation before me.'
This is what the LORD says:
'Only if the heavens above can be measured
and the foundations of the earth below be searched out
will I reject all the descendants of Israel because of all they have done.'

There's still more. A striking thing about Old Testament prophecy is the way in which the glorious end-time blessing is described as centred very concretely on the *land* of Israel. To pick just a few of many examples that are worth turning up, we can look at Isaiah 2:1-4, or the end of Amos, or the end of Obadiah which is very specific about the areas of the land that are in view.[11] Again, it's hard to see how, if we've read the whole of Amos or Obadiah, the 'joyful turn' of the final verses can be meaningful unless it has a fulfilment in ethnic Israel. We should look at Zechariah 2, which states clearly, 'Many nations will be joined with the LORD in that day and will become my people' (v11), then adds equally clearly in the following verse, 'The LORD will inherit Judah ... *in the holy land* (emphasis mine) and will again choose Jerusalem.' And then there are the last chapters of Zechariah, which focus on a concrete description of a terrible physical conflict centred on Jerusalem (reminiscent again of Matthew 24:15-22), a conflict which is the immediate precursor to the Lord's return to the Mount of Olives in physical form (Zechariah 14:4); and then comes, not the end of the planet, but an era of universal worship centred on the city of Jerusalem (14:16-21).

But the hardest book to grasp or preach, it seems to me, unless you believe in God having an end-time future for ethnic (twelve-tribe) Israel including a rebuilt temple, must be the entire last quarter of Ezekiel, from chapter 36 to chapter 48. The section starts with a prophecy explicitly linked geographically to 'the mountains of Israel ... the ravines and valleys' (36:1,4). Then comes the famous vision of the valley of dry bones in chapter 37, surely also (primarily) about ethnic Israel:

> Then you, my people, will know that I am the LORD, when I open your graves and bring you up from them. I will put my Spirit in you and you will live, and I will settle you *in your own land*. *(Emphasis mine)*

But as we read the still-unfulfilled prophecy of the reunification of Ephraim (the lost northern tribes) with Judah (37:15-22), we know we must be dealing with the end times. Then in the next two chapters, God's dramatic judgement on the invaders 'from the far north' also seems to present events there in the land of Palestine as central to the end times.[12] It's specifically through this judgement – likewise unfulfilled in history so far – that God's self-revelation is recognised decisively by 'many nations'

(38:23; 39:6-7,23); and the section leads up to the repeated promise:

> 'Though I sent [Israel] into exile among the nations, I will gather them *to their own land*, not leaving any behind. I will no longer hide my face from them, for I will pour out my Spirit on the house of Israel.'
>
> *Ezekiel 39:28-29 (emphasis mine)*

Most importantly, Ezekiel goes on to devote several complete chapters to details and measurements of the rebuilt temple that are surely very hard to preach in a symbolic (ie non-literal) manner by applying them to the Church.[13] Then God's visible presence returns to Jerusalem (43:2-5); and finally Ezekiel rounds off his book with a chapter prophesying the (also as yet unfulfilled) division of the land of Palestine, not among Judah alone but among all the tribes of Israel, including those long-lost northerners.

What can all these chapters be but a prophecy of the end time, and of ethnic Israel's crucial place in it?

Ethnic Israel in the New Testament

It's important for us to recognise that in the New Testament too, God's people among the ethnic Jews and their land once again become central to God's purposes as the final drama develops.

We've already seen this in Romans 11's depiction of God's end-time plan for ethnic Israel to bring life to the world; and in the way Paul, writing in a thoroughly non-apocalyptic way about the end times in 2 Thessalonians 2:3-4, speaks of a crucial sign of the end when the final dictator sets himself up to be worshipped in God's temple in Jerusalem. We see it also in the Gospels, in Jesus' deep concern in Matthew 24 to forewarn those living in Judaea (v16; and keeping the Sabbath meticulously, v20) about events which do seem to be part of the final crisis (vv14,21-22,29).[14] (And this is in a context where Jesus clearly knows He will be rejected by the Jews [23:37]; their role in the events preceding His second coming is not conditional on what they did during His first.) We see it also notably in His answer in Acts 1:6-7: the disciples ask Jesus when He will 'restore the kingdom to Israel' (which they anyway would surely have understood in physical terms). His reply is not that they have misunderstood things and this is not what will happen, but specifically that it is not for them to know the times or dates (v7).

As we might expect, we see a clear emphasis on ethnic Israel and its land in Revelation. Revelation 7:3-8 explicitly presents members of the twelve historic Israelite tribes (including the lost northern ones) having some crucial role, which is contrasted with the people 'from *every* nation, tribe, people and language' (emphasis mine) introduced in verse 9 as soon as the list of Israelite tribes is over.[15] Revelation 11:1-3 presents the forty-two month (1,260-day) crisis as a period when the 'Gentiles' will trample on the 'holy city' and its temple. Revelation 16:12,16 presents matters coming to climax as the Animal and the armies of all the nations gather for battle in the land of Israel.[16] (Just listing these reminds me again of the reasons for feeling that the more 'literal' approach makes fascinating sense of the most biblical data. My experience is that the more 'literally minded' writers tend to find these passages exciting, Revelation particularly, whereas their 'non-literal' siblings often spend their time describing how difficult and puzzling they are!)

In both the Old and New Testament, then, we see a clear flavour of 'Jewishness', a clear place for ethnic Israel, in the events of the end times. Some of us might feel this has implications for what we discussed in the previous chapter: if Christ's followers among the Jews are so central to the final crisis and its aftermath, this may strengthen the case for thinking the global Church may have been snatched away in the 'rapture' before the Animal's final onslaught. In the next chapter we'll set out further the implications for what happens after that onslaught, after Christ's triumphant return: Christ's followers among the Jews seem to have a special destiny. But first: so, surely, do the godly expressions of each and every nation! – Egypt and Iraq (Isaiah 19:24-25), the Czech Moravians and Danes whom God used to kick-start the modern missionary movement, and the different nations who later have picked up the baton. But then we ask: What about the Palestinians?

It is tragic to see Bible Christians making the mistake of thinking that the 'Jewishness' of some of God's purposes in the future justifies anything at all that the government of Israel may do in the present. A key point of the story of Abraham and Hagar (Genesis 16) is that it's disastrous to attempt to bring about God's purposes by means and methods that are not His. God loves Israel – and He loves the Palestinians too, infinitely. (See Leviticus 19:34: 'The alien living with you must be treated as one of your native-born. Love him as yourself.') As Bible Christians, compelled by the love of Jesus, social justice and the needs of others are our business. That does include the rights of the Palestinians.

But now let's repeat: equally godly Bible Christians disagree about what we've discussed in this chapter. What we're doing in this book is setting out the more 'literal' way of understanding it all, and describing how it makes sense of the biblical data. So then: what is all that about the golden age to come, the 'millennium'?

This surely is major enough to deserve a fresh chapter ...

Notes

[1] J A Thompson, *Deuteronomy* (Inter-Varsity Press, 1974), pp148-49.

[2] Alec Motyer, *The Message of James* (Inter-Varsity Press, 1985), p24.

[3] See the masterly commentary on Romans by Douglas Moo in the *New International Commentary on the New Testament* series (Eerdmans, 1996), particularly pp712-13 and 724.

[4] One cannot help noticing, for example, the minimal treatment of the very relevant closing chapters of both Ezekiel and Zechariah in both of the respected non-literalist writers Sam Storms (*Kingdom Come*) and Kim Riddlebarger (*A Case for Amillennialism*).

[5] The 'secret things' make Deuteronomy 30 an amazing chapter. Verses 11-16 set out clearly the Old Testament's upfront 'deal' between God and Israel where salvation is earned through keeping the law. But the rest of the Old Testament experience shows us the vital lesson that humanity needed to be taught about religion and faith: we can never get God's blessing by earning it like that, but only by grace. And once that learning experience had been lived out and recorded for the sake of all humankind, in Romans 10:5-9 the Holy Spirit returns to these verses and footnotes them remarkably with something unexpected, revealing the 'secret things that belong to the Lord' and explaining the way to God that brings life: it's about Christ, His death, and how we are saved by responding to Him. The 'secret things belong to the Lord', says Deuteronomy 29:29; and by the footnoting to Deuteronomy that He provides in Romans 10, God reveals them. Glorious!

[6] Alec Motyer, *Isaiah* (Inter-Varsity Press, 1999), p117.

[7] Tom Wright, *Justification* (SPCK, 2009), p40. Of course, the gloriously liberating arrangements of jubilee (Leviticus 25) meant that the Jewish mind was accustomed to thinking in terms of 'sevens' or 'weeks' of years, as Riddlebarger rightly observes (p179). On the remarkable accuracy of the timing of this prediction, see chapter 9 of John Lennox's superb book on Daniel, *Against the Flow* (Monarch, 2015).

[8] In *Jesus and the Restoration of Israel*, ed Carey Newman, p257.

[9] I'm saving a difficult but important issue here for these endnotes. Obviously Jerusalem wasn't destroyed within seven years of Christ's being 'cut off' – it was nearly forty years later – and there is more that happens after that in verse 27. But various writers have noticed how this and a good number of other passages make most sense if we postulate that, when (at Calvary, then again in Acts) the Jews rejected God's offer of great blessing and indeed crucified their Messiah, the 'prophetic clock' of God's purposes for them 'stopped ticking'; there was a 'hiatus', a 'parenthesis'. Here in Daniel 9 that parenthesis would happen between the sixty-ninth 'week of years' when Christ is 'cut off', and the seventieth when the Jews and their city take centre stage in God's purposes again (as the 'times of the Gentiles' draw to a close: Luke 21:24; Romans 11:15,25). The parenthesis suggestion can be justified by how it helps make sense of several other puzzling passages: for example, the sudden shift from known historical events in Daniel 11:1-32 to unfulfilled prophecies about the 'time of the end' in verses 36-45, featuring a dictator described (v36) in the same terms as the end-time Animal of 2 Thessalonians 2:4; the transition from four empires of biblical times in the first part of Daniel 7 to (apparently) the end times at some later point in that chapter; and, in the New Testament, the way in which, after Israel rejected the gospel, what Peter confidently asserted 'all the prophets' had predicted concerning '*these* days' (Acts 3:24, emphasis mine) ground to a halt until the end times. It's a

suggestion that may also help us with Isaiah 61:2, or Matthew 24.

[10] And there's more. Note also Daniel 7:25, where in the crucial three-and-a-half-year period what the end-time dictator does is seek to 'change the set times and the laws', something that would not matter to Gentile Christians but might well to end-time Messianic Jews; and Daniel 11:36-45, an account of geopolitical events still unfulfilled and 'at the time of the end' (v40), in which the land of Israel is the centre of the storm.

[11] The details at the end of Obadiah, and the end of Ezekiel, as to how the inherited land will be subdivided, surely in their careful specificity demolish the common idea that the land is only promised to Israel because of its immaturity, and Israel will eventually rejoice to find that the promise's fulfilment is something far bigger than anything to do with the land at all. A father promising his immature children something of this kind, that bears no real relation to the promise's actual fulfilment, surely doesn't go into this kind of detail.

[12] I say 'seems', because it's possible that these chapters describe the same events as the attack at the end of the millennium in Revelation 20:8 (cf Storms, p434). But it's hard to see how the seven months burying corpses of Ezekiel 39:14, or the seven years using up the invaders' fuel in 39:9, can happen after Revelation 20:9. More probably, the rebels of Revelation 20 are deliberately self-identifying with the earlier invasion; and Satan's tactics haven't changed.

[13] They also don't really fit Storms' idea (drawn from Hoekema) that the Old Testament prophecies to Israel will be fulfilled, not in a future millennium, but on the new earth (pp208-09). Revelation 21:22 makes the point explicitly that there is no temple in the eternal state, 'because the Lord God Almighty and the Lamb are its temple'.

[14] See Appendix A on Matthew 24. Verse 20 is a strikingly difficult verse, because whether it refers to AD70 or the end times, no believer in either period was or will be under law about the Sabbath; see Colossians 2:16. Then again, of course, this isn't about having to break God's law or die at the hand of the invader; breaking the Sabbath had always been acceptable when the 'ox was down the well' (see Luke 14:5). Possibly what we have here is messianic Jews taking the Sabbath very seriously, but for purely cultural or heritage reasons. (This is what the Recabites were commended for in Jeremiah 35, though their unyielding teetotalism was likewise not a universal law. And compare Acts 21:24.) France (*Matthew* [Inter-Varsity Press, 1985], p341) sees this as AD70, when 'on a sabbath gates would be shut and provisions unobtainable', but it seems unlikely that that would still have been an issue when the Roman invaders were on the doorstep.

[15] It surely makes most sense, given the way the tribes are spelled out, to understand this first group as literal ethnic Israel? The long list of tribes seems bizarrely irrelevant if it is really the Church.

[16] A slightly more obscure example could be the 'woman' crowned with twelve stars who is at the centre of the events of Revelation 12. Since she apparently gives birth to Christ (v5, cf Micah 5:2-3), it may seem reasonable to identify her as godly ethnic Israel. Then the clear distinction between her and the 'rest of her offspring … who … hold to the testimony of Jesus', and whom the dragon starts to persecute worldwide by raising up the Animal (12:17–13:1,13:7), makes complete sense as the distinction between Israel as God's people and her Gentile offspring. But in that case we should again note the key place godly Israel has in the climactic 1,260-day crisis (vv6,14), and the way she is protected by fleeing to the desert (what meaning could we usefully give to that other than the literal?), as Jesus instructed them in Matthew 24:16.

Chapter Five

So What Happens After Jesus Returns?

The wolf will live with the lamb,
the leopard will lie down with the goat,
the calf and the lion and the yearling together;
and a little child will lead them.
The cow will feed with the bear,
their young will lie down together,
and the lion will eat straw like the ox.
The infant will play near the hole of the cobra,
and the young child will put [its] hand into the viper's nest.
They will neither harm nor destroy
on all my holy mountain,
for the earth will be full of the knowledge of the LORD
as the waters cover the sea.
(Isaiah 11:6-9)

Of every earthly plan that be known to man, He is
unconcerned:
He's got plans of His own to set up His throne
When He returns
(Bob Dylan, 'When He Returns', the closing words of Slow
Train Coming)[1]

Like we said: Jesus returns. And then the world is transformed.
A glorious, joyous new age, a true 'golden age', begins. What will
it be like? (And what's all that about a wonderful 'millennium'
to come on earth? Will there be such a thing?)

And, as we also just said, equally godly Christians disagree about this. What we're doing in this book is setting out the more 'literal' way of understanding it all, and how it makes sense of the biblical data.

So, Revelation. From maybe chapter 8 through to Jesus' triumphant appearance at the end of chapter 19, we read of that brief period when God allows us to learn what rejection of His reign really means, the ultimate revelation of the cost of wilful independence from God: the earth poisoned, horrific slaughter in global warfare, famine, disease, and the totalitarian rule of the ultimate dictator as Satan's final assault is embodied in the rise of the Animal, whose image must be worshipped on pain of death (13:15).[2] By chapter 16 'the kings of the whole world' have been gathered, in Palestine, for 'the battle on the great day of God Almighty'. At the end of these chapters, the end of chapter 19, God says, 'Enough.' Jesus rides out of heaven, returning to earth as King of kings. The 'kings of the earth and their armies' unite under the Animal to fight Him, but their rebellion is futile and catastrophic; the Lord reigns (19:19-21). *Hallelujah!*

Zechariah 12–14 seems to present the same horrendous events. 'All the nations of the earth' are gathered against Jerusalem (12:3); two-thirds of the Jews are being slaughtered (13:8); Jerusalem itself 'will be captured, the houses ransacked, and the women raped' (14:2). It is the final crisis of the final crisis. But as a minority of Israel calls on the Lord for rescue, He answers (13:9): God says, again, '*Enough!*' 'Then the LORD will go out and fight against those nations, as he fights in the day of battle. On that day his feet will stand on the Mount of Olives' (14:3). Just as the angels predicted in Acts 1, 'this same Jesus' has come back 'in the same way [His disciples had] seen him go into heaven', and to the same place (Acts 1:12). The inhabitants of Jerusalem:

> will look on me, the one they have pierced, and they will mourn for him as one mourns for an only child, and grieve bitterly for him as one grieves for a first-born son ... On that day a fountain will be opened to the house of David and the inhabitants of Jerusalem, to cleanse them from sin and impurity.
> *Zechariah 12:10; 13:1*

And from then on 'The LORD will be king over the whole earth' (14:9).

But what happens after that?

Obviously a good place to start looking for answers as to what comes after Revelation 19 might be Revelation 20! Chapter 20 describes 1,000 years – the 'millennium' – when

Satan is bound, 'to keep him from deceiving the nations any more until the thousand years were ended' (20:2), while the people who have been martyred because of their refusal to worship the Animal come to life and reign with Christ for the 1,000 years (20:4). Those who take the more 'literal' approach, that Christ's second coming leads into all this – alas, perhaps we do now have to use that destructive word '*pre*-millennialists' – see this as a truly golden age, when for 1,000 years this world is freed from Satan's works, and becomes, thrillingly, everything it was created for.[3] (Papias, who lived around AD60 to 130 and was in direct contact with those who heard Christ and the apostles, and who may himself have been a disciple of John, the author of Revelation, stated that 'the Lord used to teach concerning those [end] times [that] there will be a period of a thousand years after the resurrection of the dead, and the kingdom of Christ will be set up in material form on this very earth'.[4])

In other words, importantly, Satan doesn't win even in this world; on this planet, and not only by the coming of a new earth, the triumph of God will be made fully manifest. 'God didn't create the earth to simply screw it up like a piece of paper and throw it away,' writes charismatic father-figure Roger Forster, explaining why he is 'staunchly pre-millennialist'.[5] Satan will never be able to say to Christ, 'But that beautiful world, at least, I ruined permanently; you never got it back.' This earth, *this* one, will become a paradise! – one where the wolf lies down with the lamb, and the earth is full of the knowledge of the Lord as the waters cover the sea. (See such prophecies as Isaiah 11:1-12; it's important to grasp that this isn't just a vision in Revelation 20.) Jesus comes back as King, and all heaven breaks loose!

Now, Bible Christians who are less 'literalist' in these matters – 'amillennialists', to use the technical term one more time – view Revelation 20 differently. They mostly see Revelation as doubling back at this point (which is something it probably does elsewhere,[6] eg at 12:1), to history's central event: Christ's triumph through the cross. They link the binding of Satan in 20:2 (by an angel, it must be noted) to Matthew 12:28-29, where Christ explains that to liberate Satan's captives, He must first 'bind the strong man'; and then to the indisputable effects of Christ's triumph over Satan during His ministry on earth, and above all through Calvary (John 12:31; Colossians 2:15; Hebrews 2:14). Many amillennialists, therefore, read 20:4:

> I saw thrones on which were seated those who had been given authority to judge. And I saw the souls of those who had been beheaded because of their testimony for Jesus and because of the word of God. They had not worshipped the beast [the Animal] or his image and had not received his mark on their foreheads or their hands. They came to life and reigned with Christ for a thousand years

as a glorious picture of the Church's authority in Christ now that Satan is bound (or 'driven out', John 12:31, which could parallel Satan being 'locked' out in Revelation 20:3); now that 'All authority in heaven and on earth has been given to' Jesus (Matthew 28:18), and hence to us as we share His throne (Revelation 3:21).[7] (Those of us who take a different perspective should pause here to taste the sheer glory of this interpretation!) And so Revelation 20 is *now*; and although there may still be a final rebellion at the End (20:7-9), no future 'golden age' follows it in this world.[8] The Jews' rejection of Christ has meant that God's promises to them find fulfilment in Christ and the Church as the new Israel, and therefore are reinterpreted with *solely* a spiritual rather than *also* a physical fulfilment. After our present age is over we move straight into the final judgement and the coming of the new heaven and new earth (20:11-21:1).[9]

Either interpretation – Christ returning triumphantly as King to turn the earth, literally, into the paradise it was first created to be; or Christ reigning invisibly but absolutely now, and delegating His authority over Satan to us – offers us tremendous encouragement. But (leaving aside for the moment all the passages we've been feeding on about God's promises for the ethnic Jews), the question here is: Which approach seems to match most tightly with what Revelation 20 actually says?

And here, it seems to me, what we've been calling the more 'literal' approach repeatedly scores most highly:

1. Accepting that Revelation's narrative does sometimes 'double back', surely it is not doing so here. The people who '[come] to life and [reign] with Christ for a thousand years' are specifically those who have not worshipped the Animal or its image and have not received its mark on their foreheads or their hands. This means we are looking at a time later than the horrific end-time events of chapter 13 (and 2 Thessalonians 2:4), a time later than the emergence of the Animal for (13:5) the final crisis of history.[10] When chapter 20 comes that crisis is over; the Animal has been

finally defeated with Christ's open return as King in 19:20. It's after this climax of the end time that the believers the Animal has martyred come to life and reign for a thousand years.

2. Again, Revelation 20:10 clearly follows on and completes the judgement of Revelation 19:20. In 19:20 the Animal and his false prophet have been thrown into the lake of fire, and then in 20:10 we are explicitly told that Satan joins them there where they '*had* been thrown' (emphasis mine); the two judgements aren't simultaneous. So the first two evil beings are judged at the time of Christ's open return as King in 19:20, but the final judgement of Satan himself takes place significantly later than that; and Revelation 20 surely reads as if the millennium happens between the two.

3. Why are there the repeated references to the 'thousand years' at all (vv2,3,4,5,6,7), if they refer to our present era? The respected 'non-literalist' writer Hoekema sees these references as standing for 'a very long period of indeterminate length'.[11] But given how important it seems to be that we shouldn't know how long our present era is and how long the time before the second coming may be (so that even Jesus chose to share our ignorance, Matthew 24:36), what sense does it make (what does it add) to state any length for it at all? Unless, of course, that 1,000 years is quite literal?

4. A 'non-literalist' like Storms must see the events of 20:7-9 as the final crisis of our present era.[12] But are we to see all the horrific judgements of the forty-two-month crisis happening during these verses? Also, this means that Satan's being released from the abyss in 20:7 equals his

111

being cast out of heaven (likewise triggering the start of that crisis) in 12:8-9,13. Being released from the abyss equals being cast out of heaven – that seems very odd indeed.

5. But for me, the biggest problem is the most obvious: however can we see our present era as a time when Satan is kept 'from deceiving the nations any more', as Revelation 20:3 puts it? 'Your enemy the devil prowls around like a roaring lion looking for someone to devour', says 1 Peter 5:8; beware of Satan tempting us, says 1 Corinthians 7:5; Satan is 'the spirit who is *now* at work in those who are disobedient', says Ephesians 2:2 (emphasis mine); as the 'god of this age' (a highly noteworthy phrase in this connection!), Satan has 'blinded the minds of unbelievers, so that they cannot see the light of the gospel' (2 Corinthians 4:4).[13] In Revelation 20:3, in contrast, Mounce notes, 'The abyss is *sealed* (cf Dan 6:17, Matt 27:66) as a special precaution against escape' (emphasis mine); so that as premillennialist Wayne Grudem puts it, Revelation 20:3's reference to Satan being 'locked and sealed' away surely 'gives a picture of total removal from influence on the earth.'[14] How then can Revelation 20:2-3 be referring to our present era and our situation now?

In short, then, Revelation 20 seems to make most sense as describing what happens after Jesus returns, overthrowing the Animal and starting to reign openly as King, in chapter 19. 'Your will be done on earth as it is in heaven', we pray: now it happens! There is indeed a golden age on earth; a key part is played by those martyred by the Animal (20:4); and it is centred on Jerusalem, the 'city [God] loves' (and which Satan tries to destroy in his final rebellion before the last judgement, 20:9).

But of course we do not come to this conclusion merely because of Revelation 20, but because of what we read throughout the Bible. There's Isaiah 11 where the time when God is bringing His people back to Israel 'a second time' from the ends of the earth, 'from Cush, from Elam, from Babylonia, from Hamath and from the islands of the sea' (vv11-16) is also 'that day' when 'The wolf will live with the lamb ... They will neither harm nor destroy on all my holy mountain, for the earth will be full of the knowledge of the LORD' (vv6,9).[15] And there's Isaiah 65:20-25 where we read of a renewed earthly paradise that is yet one where death is rare but possible (unlike the eternal 'new heaven and new earth' from which death has vanished, Revelation 21:4). Psalm 72:5-11 describes the messianic King who will rule 'as long as the sun ... from the River to the ends of the earth. The desert tribes will bow before him and his enemies will lick the dust. The kings of ... distant shores will bring tribute to him' (again this doesn't sound quite like the situation in eternity?). In Zechariah 9:10, the messianic King will 'take away ... the war-horses from Jerusalem, and the battle-bow will be broken. He will proclaim peace to the nations. His rule will extend from sea to sea'. And in the closing chapter of Zechariah, after the final conflict and the second coming the Lord is reigning, but again sin and rebellion are still possible so there need to be clear sanctions against the 'survivors from all the nations that ... attacked Jerusalem' if they refuse to worship Him there (14:16-19; see also Isaiah 60:10-12). Plus we have all those many other passages – eg Deuteronomy 30, Isaiah 2 and 60, Jeremiah 3, Joel 3, Amos 9, Obadiah, Micah 4 and 7, Zechariah 2, Romans 11 – which present huge blessing to ethnic Israel as a key component of what happens at the End. And most clearly of all, it's because of the long prophecy of Ezekiel 40 to 48, which seems so strange if it is to be spiritualised and only means that 'God will have a House in the Church and that will be great', rather than what it actually says, that the temple of the Lord will be restored in Jerusalem (chs 40–42), the glory of the Lord will return there physically (chapter 43), and life, a power of literal life, will flow gloriously out of it, life flooding out in rejuvenation to all the dead lands (chapter 47)!

So what will happen in the time after Jesus returns?

It will be amazing beyond our wildest dreams! The creation, which for so long has been 'subjected to frustration' and 'groaning as in the pains of childbirth', will be joyfully 'liberated from its bondage to decay', exults Paul (Romans 8:20-22):[16]

> The wolf will live with the lamb,
> the leopard will lie down with the goat,
> the calf and the lion and the yearling together;
> and a little child will lead them.
> The cow will feed with the bear,
> their young will lie down together,
> and the lion will eat straw like the ox.
> The infant will play near the hole of the cobra,

and the young child will put [its] hand into the
viper's nest.
They will neither harm nor destroy
on all my holy mountain,
for the earth will be full of the knowledge of the
LORD
as the waters cover the sea.
Isaiah 11:6-9

Is a physical millennium, a paradise on earth, a climax
or an anticlimax after what we have of God's kingdom
now? I suggest it's a climax of the kind C S Lewis and J R R
Tolkien enthused about, where in the End of the ages
'myth' (the hidden, the symbolic, the spiritual) becomes
clothed, visibly expressed at last, in the physical. (See
Tolkien's *Tree and Leaf.*) Probably a feature of this recreated
world after Christ's return will be that the physical
expresses the spiritual in a way it seldom does now. So
although Ezekiel's river in the wonderful chapter 47 is a
great picture of life and healing flowing out of God's house
(and by glorious implication, of how life can flow out into
all the deadlands of society from His Church now [John
7:38]), isn't the most reasonable primary reading, given
how literal are the rest of Ezekiel's details (all those careful
temple measurements), that, after God's glory returns
there, the river that flows out from the temple will carry
literal life?

> I saw a great number of trees on each side of the
> river. He said to me ... 'When it empties into the
> [Dead] Sea, the water there becomes fresh.
> Swarms of living creatures will live wherever the

river flows. There will be large numbers of fish,
because this water flows there and makes the salt
water fresh; so where the river flows everything
will live. Fishermen will stand along the shore ...'

(Read Ezekiel 47:1-12; it's tremendous!) Somehow the bringing of all this *'life from the dead'* to a hugely damaged world will involve the Jewish followers of Jesus (returning to Romans 11:15); and Paul says this will amount (amazingly and almost inconceivably) to blessing greater even than salvation extending to the Gentiles in his lifetime (11:12)![17]

> Till the Spirit is poured on us from on high,
> and the desert becomes a fertile field,
> and the fertile field seems like a forest ...
> The desert and the parched land will be glad;
> the wilderness will rejoice and blossom.
> Like the crocus, it will burst into bloom;
> it will rejoice greatly and shout for joy.
> *Isaiah 32:15; 35:1-2*

'Sit enthroned, O Jerusalem', says Isaiah 52:2; Jerusalem will be, as Jesus said, 'the city of the Great King' (Matthew 5:35; what could He be referring to but this, when He Himself will reign over the earth from there?[18])

And with the Lord reigning in Jerusalem, what will that mean for worship? Isaiah 2:2-4 says clearly:

> In the last days,
> the mountain of the LORD's temple will be
> established
> as chief among the mountains;

it will be raised above the hills,
and all nations will stream to it.
Many peoples will come and say,
'Come, let us go up to the mountain of the LORD,
to the house of the God of Jacob.
He will teach us his ways,
so that we may walk in his paths.'
The law will go out from Zion,
the word of the LORD from Jerusalem.
He will judge between the nations
and will settle disputes for many peoples.
They will beat their swords into ploughshares
and their spears into pruning hooks.
Nation will not take up sword against nation,
nor will they train for war any more.

(It's the situation that was foreshadowed briefly with Solomon and the Queen of Sheba, but this time it's permanent. However, a situation where there are disputes to be settled is obviously something other than that of eternity.)[19] The last five verses of Zechariah make clear that 'going up to Jerusalem to worship the King' will be central to that era's spirituality; and so does Jeremiah 3:17: 'At that time they will call Jerusalem The Throne of the LORD, and all nations will gather in Jerusalem to honour the name of the LORD'! (Amen! Hallelujah!)

(One reaction one often hears to all this is: But how can any system of temple sacrifices be instituted again, as Ezekiel 44-46 – and Jeremiah 33:18 and Zechariah 14:21 – indicate? Wouldn't this be regressing back to the Old Testament era? And obviously [this is the point of Hebrews 10] there could never be any idea of sacrifices that in any sense could 'take away sins' [Hebrews 10:4,11,18]. But perhaps it should not surprise us if after the second coming, in this centre of global worship [Zechariah 14:16-19], Christ's death is remembered through the symbolism of animal sacrifices, the grim bloodshed of which illustrates so powerfully the horrific cost of our sin, and the colossal price Christ paid for us. [After all, Paul tells us that by taking the symbols of the bread and wine we 'proclaim the Lord's death *until* he comes' (1 Corinthians 11:26, emphasis mine)!] In an almost exact parallel, the bread and wine now do not 'take away sins': they too are given to us as a powerful reminder of the cross, which did. In the millennium, it may seem, a different reminder will be given to us.)

And what about everyday life? Here Scripture cannot tell us much, given that the new age obviously follows upon one as developed (at least) as our own, where everyday life has cultural forms unimaginable to the biblical writers. But I loved the speculations in the chapter titled 'The Redemption of London' in Andrew Wilson's superb apologetics book *If God, Then What?*:

> People in the redeemed London live without anything to prove, in complete security, and this has all sorts of implications that make it hard to recognise as London ... People on the Tube make eye contact with one another and smile, instead of hiding behind their newspapers, because now strangers are not people to be avoided because they're all scary, but people to be celebrated because they are all happy ... The roads are weird: taxis don't cut one another up around

Parliament Square or Hyde Park Corner, nobody honks their horn in frustration, bus drivers look happy, and you can't hear any sirens … *Metro* doesn't have any negative stories anymore, and nobody kills or abuses or cheats on any one … The oddest thing about the redemption of London is the way people work … People still work, but they do it not so much for their own benefit as for the whole community. The City is still there, but all the financial whizz-kids spend their best years trying to work out how to use money to help the most people. All the advertising agencies up by Goodge Street use their creativity and communication skills to praise what is honourable and admirable for its own sake. Oxford Street, would you believe, has become a massive open-air market, where every product you can find is crafted with care … Every square inch of the city has had the good reinforced, and the bad removed, and it spills over into the arts scene, the architecture, the public spaces, even the government. It's a sight to see.[20]

(Ironically, I understand Wilson himself wouldn't hold to the approach we're setting out in this book, but his chapter is a glorious response to this question nonetheless.)

Whatever it's like, the new age is going to be made wonderful beyond belief! Thank You, Jesus!

But here's the thing, and this is why this book has one more chapter to go: What God has prepared for us in eternity – when 'the mortal' has finally been 'clothed …

with immortality', gloriously 'swallowed up by life' (1 Corinthians 15:53; 2 Corinthians 5:4) – is unimaginably better still!

And now an important PS...

One thing I'm looking forward to when I get to heaven is learning what I was wrong about!

I know I won't be wrong about Jesus being God, or about Him dying to pay for our sins according to the Scriptures – the kind of things 1 Corinthians 15:3 calls 'of first importance'. But I may well find my sisters and brothers were right and I was wrong about, say, the charismatic gift of prophecy, or election and free will, or what does and does not grieve the Spirit about women's ministry: things that equally godly Bible Christians see differently. The approach set out in this chapter is like that. It may very well be wrong!

It's true too that the viewpoint set out here is very much a minority one, at least on this side of the Atlantic. But that doesn't necessarily mean it's wrong. Early in the second century AD the great apologist Justin Martyr affirmed, 'I and others are assured that there will be a resurrection of the dead and a thousand years in Jerusalem, which will then be built, adorned and enlarged', while recognising that 'many who are true Christians think otherwise.'[21] (The 'others' from the second century that we know about who awaited the millennial transformation of the natural world included the author of the *Epistle to Barnabas*, and Papias, Irenaeus and Tertullian.) Again, second-century believers went thoroughly astray on other things. Nevertheless, it's a shame that this whole perspective is almost forgotten in our own country and era; we may very well come to need it.

So that's why this book was written!

Notes

1 From 'When He Returns'. Copyright © 1979 by Special Rider Music. All rights reserved. International copyright secured. Reprinted by permission.

2 Matthew 24:22 is very interesting here: 'If those days' (the 'great distress, unequalled from the beginning of the world', v21) 'had not been cut short, no-one would survive.' So the issue determining that God steps in to 'cut short' this terrible time is that otherwise no one would be left alive on earth. But that raises a striking question: if, as 'non-literalists' say, there were no millennium on earth to follow, and this world were about to end anyway, why would this matter?

3 It is 'the day of the greatest glory for the world', William Kelly, *Lectures on the Book of the Revelation* (A S Rouse, 1893), p443.

4 Quoted by John Warwick Montgomery in *Handbook of Biblical Prophecy*, ed Carl Armerding and Ward Gasque (Baker, 1977), p177.

5 In *Doing a New Thing?*, ed Brian Hewitt (Hodder, 1995), p126. It's worth noting that Roger Forster has been one of Britain's most motivational teachers of how we can bring in God's kingdom *now*, of getting as much heaven on earth as possible *now*: see his book *The Kingdom of Jesus* (Authentic, 2002). Premillennialism certainly need not contradict that vision, despite what's sometimes suggested.

6 Revelation's three sequences of seven judgements – seven seals, seven trumpets, seven bowls – don't overlap entirely, but all apparently culminate in a climax of 'earthquake, thunder and hail' (6:12-17; 11:15-19; 16:17-21) that seems to mark the End; after which the narrative recommences.

7 There is an alternative amillennialist interpretation, where

those martyred by antichrist forces throughout the Christian era have been raised *spiritually* and are reigning now, not on earth, but in the supernatural universe. Sam Storms affirms this by arguing (*Kingdom Come*, p458) that Revelation 20:4 parallels the words of Revelation 6:9-11, and notes particularly the reference to the martyrs' 'souls' being what is seen, in both cases. But: 1) Isn't 'reigning' an extremely odd description for what is happening in 6:9-11? – odd enough to make a clear distinction between the martyrs' situation in chapter 6 and their reigning at a different time in chapter 20? Furthermore, the place in the early chapters where we read about God's people reigning is Revelation 5:10, and there it is explicitly 'on the earth'. 2) 'Came to life' and 'resurrection' (Revelation 20:4,6) seem somewhat strange ways for John to describe a *spiritual* resurrection that happens to the martyrs, since, as far as the supernatural universe is concerned, these believers had surely 'come to life' and been 'raised with Christ' ever since they were born again (John 5:24, Ephesians 2:5-6)? 3) Both the verb's other uses in Revelation, 2:8 and 13:14, apply to a physical resurrection. 4) Arguably, John says 'souls' here precisely because he then watched these people 'come to life', ie in a physical resurrection. 5) The 'rest of the dead' 'come to life' in verse 5, and since they (or many of them) are unbelievers this certainly is not a spiritual but a physical resurrection; why then should the 'resurrection' of the martyrs in the previous verse be any different? So Storms' suggestion seems improbable.

[8] For me, the strongest of Storms' arguments against a literal, this-worldly millennial kingdom in chapter 5 of *Kingdom Come* is when he draws upon 1 Corinthians 15:50: 'I declare to you, brothers, that flesh and blood cannot inherit the kingdom of God'. But we must all agree that the biblical phrase 'kingdom of God' refers to something that comes in stages, starting clearly within this very 'flesh-and-blood' world in the Gospels (see Matthew 11:12; 12:28; Mark 1:15; 9:1, and indeed Paul's own

words in Romans 14:17 and 1 Corinthians 4:20); even though equally it sometimes refers to the future (eg Luke 13:28-29). In Matthew 21:31 'the tax collectors and the prostitutes' (flesh and blood, presumably) 'are entering the kingdom of God'; Paul himself is joyfully announcing the kingdom's arrival on earth while still very much in the body in the closing verse of Acts. It seems, then, that in 1 Corinthians 15:50 he happens to be using the term to refer only to the ultimate stage where we at last 'inherit' all God has for us (until then we only have a 'deposit', not the full inheritance, Ephesians 1:14); something on the way to which even the glory of the millennium is only an incomplete though wonderful stage that he passes over. Storms might argue, however, that in this case it's odd that someone as aware as Paul of God's Old Testament promises should not have felt a need to make things clearer.

[9] 2 Peter 3:10-12 does sound as if the second coming, 'that day', immediately brings the end of this cosmos when 'everything will be destroyed' – but we need to be careful what conclusions we draw from this since Peter has just said, 'With the Lord a day is like a thousand years'! If I myself were arguing the 'non-literal' case I would emphasise here Revelation 11:18, where at the end of the final crisis the elders say, 'The time has come for judging the dead'; this does sound like the great white throne at the end of the millennium, implying that the millennium is something that has come to a close by the end of chapter 11. (The reference to all those on earth seeing 'the face of him who sits on the throne' at the end of chapter 6 could support this too.) One response is that, as we will explore in the next chapter, it may well be that time viewed from heaven (eg by the heavenly elders) is rather different from time as experienced on earth; again, 'With the Lord a day is like a thousand years'! Another is that this could be referring to the judgement of Matthew 25:31, before the millennium, rather than the great white throne. Yet another is that if Revelation 12:1ff sees a

recapitulation (as most amillennialists would agree), going back to prehistory and the fall of Satan, then it is not surprising that the narrative of chapter 11 extends first to the very end of our planet's history.

[10] It's worth remembering here that even such strong proponents of the 'non-literal' approach as Kim Riddlebarger (*A Case for Amillennialism*), eg pp146,155,272, and Sam Storms (*Kingdom Come*), pp36,546-47, while recognising the 'repeated manifestation' of what the Animal represents throughout history, also look to its embodiment in the rise of a specific, ultimately evil end-time dictator.

[11] In *The Meaning of the Millennium: Four Views*, ed Robert Clouse (InterVarsity Press, 1977), p161. Hoekema adds rather confidently, 'Obviously the number "thousand" which is used here must not be interpreted in a literal sense', because 'Revelation is full of symbolic numbers.' But is it? What significant symbolism is communicated by 1,260, or forty-two, or three and a half?

[12] Cf Storms, p466.

[13] For other clear examples of Satan's deceptive activity *since* the cross see Acts 5:3, 1 Thessalonians 2:18 and 2 Timothy 2:26.

[14] Robert Mounce, commentary on Revelation in the *New International Commentary on the New Testament* series (Eerdmans, 1977), p353, my italics; Wayne Grudem, *Bible Doctrine*, p447.

[15] And how would Christ's ruling over the nations 'with an iron sceptre' (Revelation 12:5) fit into the eternal state?

[16] This is something that Storms sees as instantaneous, and therefore presents as a reason why a literal millennial age is impossible (pp137,153). But the coming of God's renewing kingdom has always been step by step, and there is no reason at all why the creation's liberation should not receive a wonderful

beginning with the advent of the millennium (Revelation 20), where the 'wolf and the lamb will feed together', and then be brought on to entire, triumphant completion with the arrival of the ultimate 'new heaven and new earth' (Revelation 21).

[17] See again Douglas Moo's commentary on Romans in the *New International Commentary on the New Testament* series, pp694-95.

[18] 'And the name of the city from that time on will be: THE LORD IS THERE' (Ezekiel's closing verse, 48:35).

[19] Compare also Joel 3, where the world of verse 18, wonderfully restored after the final battle of verses 9-16 to one where 'the mountains will drip new wine', is still one where Edom is 'a desert waste, because of violence done to the people of Judah'.

[20] Andrew Wilson, *If God, Then What?* (Inter-Varsity Press, 2012), pp121-23.

[21] Quoted by Montgomery, pp177-78.

Chapter Six

Greater Things Still! Wondering About Heaven

What's heaven like? And why wonder about heaven anyway?

Why wonder about heaven? Surely the answer's obvious: anything we'll be doing for the next million years deserves our serious attention!

But what we often forget is this: God makes clear in the New Testament that thinking about heaven is vital for our survival. The big panorama of eternity is the vital backcloth to our lives here; grasping it makes a huge difference to our spiritual growth.

We're in a continual battle to be radical disciples; radical amid all the brainwashing around us that pushes us to live and be the same way as everybody else; battling too against the temptations of the flesh, and all the malice of the devil. How do we resist? When Paul presents the vital spiritual 'armour' that protects us in this conflict, he says that our hope of our coming salvation is our 'helmet', that which protects our minds (1 Thessalonians 5:8). Our grasp of the wonder and glory of what God has got stored up for us is what will protect our thinking! 'Set your hearts on things above', he instructs the Colossians (3:1); we are meant to be 'hungry for heaven', 'longing to be clothed with our heavenly dwelling' (2 Corinthians 5:2).

Peter says the same. In both his epistles we see a clear choice set out: desire for heaven set repeatedly against the 'evil desires' of this world. '[Setting] your hope fully on the grace to be given you' is God's alternative to '[conforming] to the evil desires you had' (look at 1 Peter 1:13-14). The people who ignore the hope of the future are also the ones who 'follow their own evil desires' (2 Peter 3:3-4); it's through God's 'very great and precious promises' that we 'escape the corruption in the world caused by evil desires' (2 Peter 1:4). Our lives are shaped by what we desire; and it's one set of desires or the other.

The writer of the letter to the Hebrews likewise reminds its readers that they were able to cope with having their possessions confiscated by their persecutors precisely because of their firm grasp of the glory of heaven (10:34). And he evocatively describes our hope as an 'anchor', reaching in 'behind the curtain'(6:19); it's like a ship's anchor that fastens firmly into the invisible ocean floor, and so prevents it from being blown around, away up on the surface. Our firm imaginative grasp of what we cannot see keeps us from being shaken by the waves we can see.

So when Paul tells us that 'No eye has seen, no ear has heard, no mind has conceived what God has prepared for those who love him' (1 Corinthians 2:9), we can take it as a challenge! God wants us to begin to grasp, be thrilled by, even be armed by these things (Ephesians 1:17-18); by such faith we will live (Hebrews 10:34-38). It's not surprising that the central Christian meal, the Lord's Supper, is also, in part, future-orientated ('For whenever you eat this bread and drink this cup, you proclaim the Lord's death *until he comes*' [emphasis mine], 1 Corinthians 11:26). We need that regular stimulus to our vision. What God has prepared for us is more than we can ask or imagine (Ephesians 3:20). It's worth our chewing on that, dreaming about it, getting the glory of it into our souls... because this may prove crucial to our spiritual survival!

Grasping this priority is surely the symbolic purpose of Christ's ascension. Heaven isn't somewhere up in the sky, after all; it's a supernatural dimension that overlaps in all sorts of ways with our own. Why then did God choose for Jesus' departure to be expressed by disappearing upwards (rather than by, say, Jesus declaring, 'I am with you always,' and then just vanishing)? What important lesson does this embody? Surely it's to make the point that Jesus' being 'here still but unrevealed' is a glorious fact but is not the whole story. Rather, there's an all-important sense in which our Master, 'the one who comes from above ... not of this world' (John 3:31; 8:23), has 'gone away' (see John 14:28) somewhere better, to another dimension *'above'* (God's chosen phrasing, Colossians 3:1). And we His people belong there (Colossians 3:2-4); we are 'aliens and strangers' in this world (1 Peter 2:11), no more at home here now than Jesus was (John 17:16).

So now, even as we labour as He did to get as much heaven on earth now as possible, our deepest desires and loyalties are elsewhere. That better world with its own values is where we belong, where we're headed, and what we are to focus on above all. 'Set your minds on things above, not on earthly things', says Paul (Colossians 3:2). 'So we fix our eyes not on what is seen, but on what is unseen', he adds in 2 Corinthians 4:18. 'Enemies of the cross' live with their 'mind on earthly things. But our citizenship is in heaven. And we eagerly await a Saviour from there' (Philippians 3:19-20). 'The present heavens and earth are reserved for fire ... Since everything will be destroyed in this way, what kind of people ought you to be?' (2 Peter 3:7,11). That world, not this, is where we are meant primarily to invest our efforts and store up our treasure (Matthew 6:19-20), and our dream is 'to depart and be with Christ, which is better by far' (Philippians 1:23).

So back to Revelation then. How does it all conclude? The glorious millennial age isn't the end of the story. Instead, at its end there is a final rebellion against God (20:7-9).[1] Christ the King from heaven is again victorious; amen! But then comes the final judgement, and the catastrophic fate of hell for everyone whose name is not written in the book of life (20:15). And now there's a massive transition. The 'first heaven and the first earth' have 'passed away' (21:1). ('The heavens will disappear with a roar', writes Peter; 'the elements will be destroyed by fire ... we are looking forward to a new heaven and a new earth, the home of righteousness' [2 Peter 3:10,13].) And now God brings into being that hugely glorious 'new heaven and new earth' (Revelation 21:1).

What will this mean for us if we're followers of Jesus? It means we'll move into the life God created us for: living in His presence forever. It's hard to imagine (but worth trying!) how fantastic this will be. To repeat, 1 Corinthians

2:9 tells us that 'no mind has conceived what God has prepared for those who love him'; and Ephesians 2:7 says God plans to use the coming ages to show us just how colossally He loves us! (We can see why Titus 2:13 says that 'we wait for the blessed hope – the glorious appearing of our great God and Saviour, Jesus Christ' that will bring us into all this!) God is a God of infinite love, joy and creativity, and it's going to be glory beyond imagination to experience that fully. And as we think about Jesus' invitation to share our Master's joy (Matthew 25:21,23), we should remember again that God, as Dallas Willard says, is certainly the most joyful being in the universe! In comparison we have only tasted the slightest droplets of joy, even in our best moments here!

But there could be nothing more tragic than to miss out on this (as so many of our friends may do). This chapter is more about heaven than hell, but we need to grasp the reality of both. On both topics it's not clever to be too dogmatic, but here are some ideas and possibilities to think about.

Most of us would simply prefer that hell didn't exist. But Jesus makes clear that it does. There is His unflinching either/or in Matthew 7:13-14:

> 'Enter through the narrow gate. For wide is the gate and broad is the road that leads to destruction, and many enter through it. But small is the gate and narrow the road that leads to life, and only a few find it.'

There is His warning in the Sermon on the Mount (Matthew 5:30, and He repeats it elsewhere) that 'if your right hand causes you to sin, cut it off and throw it away. It is better for you to lose one part of your body' – really? – 'than for your whole body to go into hell.' There is a similar either/or in Matthew 25:32-34,41, where our alternative destinations are heaven or else a hellish environment not designed for humans at all. And there's His famous narrative of the rich man in hell in Luke 16:23-26.

The fact is that, whatever it's like, hell has to exist if human freedom is to be real. God doesn't rape people and force them into His presence. But Jesus makes it very clear (John 3:3): it's if we choose to live under God's kingship and to invite the life and presence of God within us now that we will have God's kingship and His life and presence then; if we choose against heaven now, we won't have heaven then. There comes a point when our life-choice becomes fixed (like Graham Greene's Bendrix at the tragic close of *The End of the Affair*), when we have rejected grace for the last time (2 Corinthians 6:1). But that is the most disastrous thing in the world.

This whole topic of hell is difficult, because often our understandings come not from the Bible but from the imaginations of the medieval Church. We can be sure that hell is not like the medieval pictures of devils toasting people with pitchforks like cheese. (In the traditions (hadiths) of our Muslim friends, by the way, hell is like that and far worse.) 2 Thessalonians 1:8-9 describes the fate of the lost as being shut out in the darkness, outside God's presence; so do Matthew 25:30 and Luke 13:24-28. Biblically, being excluded from God's presence seems basic to what hell is about.

What does that imply? There's so much we don't know. It seems reasonable to think that hell will be as merciful as a loving God can make it: God doesn't want any of us to go there, and that's why He took the quite astounding step of giving His only Son to bear hell for us on the cross. There is a real case for saying that biblically hell is eternal and conscious, but Bible Christians as firmly committed to Scripture as John Stott and Michael Green have disputed this.[2] But who knows what 'eternal and conscious' means? Perhaps time passes almost infinitely slowly there. Perhaps too, as C S Lewis suggested in *The Great Divorce* (still arguably the best book to read about hell), in hell our consciousnesses and personalities disintegrate, so that what survives there is not so much a grumbler as a grumble. It is certainly true that relationship with God is what most enhances our personalities, and perhaps the further and longer we get away from God, the more our personalities disintegrate. We see that with drug addicts: how a personality can dwindle to a craving and almost nothing more.

But still Jesus makes clear that the danger of hell is enormously, unbelievably serious. Think what it means to experience absolute separation, forever, from God's presence. God is the source of all love, all joy, all peace, all hope. So to be separated, absolutely and forever, from the presence of God is presumably to be in a state (if we can imagine it) where there is no love, no joy, no peace, no hope, and there never will be. The mind staggers before such a thought. Jesus speaks understandably of 'darkness, where there will be weeping' (Matthew 22:13). No one could imagine anything more catastrophic. God's love should motivate us each to do all we can to ensure that nobody, anywhere at all, fails to realise the huge consequences of joining their lives now to Jesus, or not. If we're separated from Jesus when we die, that means permanent, disastrous separation from Him thereafter; if we're joined to Jesus when we die, we'll be with Him forever in heaven, sharing glory beyond our wildest dreams.

The fact is that Jesus makes it clear, whether we like it or not, that there is a hell, that it's not a good place to go to, and that people like us go there. If we have any love in our hearts we must surely warn our friends – implore them, says Paul (2 Corinthians 5:20) – to repent, receive the Lord's forgiveness and be reconciled to God. Indeed if we see the *world* the way God the Father does (John 3:16), we'll know that any price is worth paying to ensure that people throughout the world can act upon God's rescuing gospel. *Let's pray that, somehow, God helps us grasp what Jesus says about the seriousness and horror of hell, and witness accordingly to the way, the only way, that our friends and colleagues can be sure to avoid going there!*

But the other place, the glorious one...

So then, heaven. So many things that happen – death, unhealed disease, unrepaired relationships – are inexplicable on earth, and make sense only when we take our training for heaven into account. In heaven we will have millions upon millions of years to harvest the benefit of what has happened here, and to use the steel that is in our souls because of tough things that happened here that could never have happened in heaven. Only in the light of this training can some of the things that occur here make any sense. It's one of the ways in which our hope of heaven is our 'anchor'.

So a few things about heaven. When we 'die and go to heaven', just where do we go?

Maybe nowhere that we haven't gone already! Above all, heaven means being with Jesus. So biblically, heaven is not where we go when we die; heaven is where we go now when we first become Christians and are born again! Paul describes our situation as believers like this: 'God ... seated us with [Christ] in the heavenly realms in Christ Jesus' (Ephesians 2:6).[3] In other words, we are already, now, 'seated with Christ' in heaven! When we were born again, we were completely united with Christ – brought definitively into His Body (1 Corinthians 12:13). Or to put it another way, God's Spirit who came to live inside us then is the 'deposit' or foretaste of heaven, as Paul keeps on saying (eg Ephesians 1:14; 2 Corinthians 5:5). From then on, heaven has a foothold or bridgehead inside us, from which its transforming powers break now into our decaying world; and one day – at death or the second coming – they will sweep through our personalities completely. But the foothold's there already. Graham Kendrick's song 'Heaven Is In My Heart' had it right! When we were born again, we entered into heaven, and heaven entered into us. We are with God, He is with us; we are 'seated' in heaven *now*!

Of course, we don't actually feel it; most of the time, anyway. Right now our five senses are firmly attuned to this world; and so – most of the time, apart from odd moments, hints, occasional glimpses in the best minutes of our lives that we sense momentarily and then they're gone – we don't actually experience heaven, our being 'seated' in total union with Christ. But that's why death will be the supreme adventure. We're like people walking through the woods wearing headphones. Outside, the birds are singing, but there's too much noise pumping into our ears, and we can't hear them at all. Then suddenly the batteries go totally dead ... and for the first time we hear what's really there! So when we close our eyes for the last time to this world, and open them to the more real, eternal universe, we shall suddenly see where we've been living – see the forces that really matter, the overwhelming universe of angels and demons, God and Satan, heaven and hell, that we've been stumbling round all this time. It will undoubtedly come as a shock. No doubt we'll ask, 'Why did I worry so much? Why was I so afraid? Why did I invest my energies the way I did?' In addition, we'll see the rest of the Body of Christ, including all our fellow-believers who have 'crossed over' earlier.

So what's it going to be like?

It's unimaginable: that much we know! There will undoubtedly be some real continuity with the best of our present world (otherwise why does Scripture speak of a new 'earth' [Revelation 21:1; 2 Peter 3:13]?) There will also clearly be a dramatic break, not just with the earth we know, but the heavens too. 'Heaven and earth will pass away', says Jesus clearly (Matthew 24:35). Peter says:

The heavens will disappear with a roar; the elements will be destroyed by fire, and the earth and everything in it will be laid bare.

Since everything will be destroyed in this way, what kind of people ought you to be? ... That day will bring about the destruction of the heavens by fire, and the elements will melt in the heat. But in keeping with his promise we are looking forward to a new heaven and a new earth, the home of righteousness.

2 Peter 3:10-13

(See also Psalm 102:26, Isaiah 51:6, and Hebrews 1:11-12.)

We cannot imagine the ways in which our glorious new home may be radically different. For instance, Jesus' laconic statement that in the world to come there is no marriage as we know it (Matthew 22:30) clearly implies, as Don Carson says, 'an existence quite unlike this present one'.[4] This does seem to undermine the currently popular idea that the eternal world is pretty much like the present one, only purged of evil. A 'new heaven' as well as a 'new earth' does sound like a radically transformed cosmos, and this new cosmos of heaven and earth may be radically different to ours in all kinds of glorious, thrilling and unimaginable ways!

Paul describes what he saw in this new cosmos that will so triumphantly replace our own as 'inexpressible things' (2 Corinthians 12:4; see also 1 Corinthians 2:9 and 1 John 3:2). And in Revelation 4 and 5 we sense John, inspired by God the Spirit, stretching language to its limits in his struggle to catch something of the wonder he's seen.

But of this much we can be sure: to be totally in the presence of God, face to face with Him at last, must be to experience the fullness of His infinite love, infinite joy, infinite peace, infinite gentleness. Heaven exists because the Lord loves us and wants our company; His longing is that we should be with Him (John 17:24; Ephesians 2:7). We've only ever caught the briefest and most limited glimpses, here on earth, of what undiluted love and joy are like. There, we're going to taste them fully. *Thank You, Lord!*

We shall experience all Christ's glory there (John 17:24): the glory Moses longed to see but was told he simply could not see and survive (Exodus 33:20); and we shall worship! We read about a fantastic worship symphony in Revelation 4, and especially 5:9-14. One day we shall see this with our own eyes! *Thank You, Lord!*

And even more amazingly, that glory will overflow into us and be *in* us (Romans 8:18)! When Christ comes back, says Paul, He will 'be glorified in' – not merely by, but in – 'his holy people' (2 Thessalonians 1:10,12). We shall look at each other and see a unique embodiment of the glory of God that He has brought to expression in us, as throughout our lives He has helped us become like Jesus. At the end of history the community of God, the collective Bride of Christ, will actually shine 'with the glory of God' (Revelation 21:11). We won't just see the glory; it will be flooding out through us. So we can look forward to knowing each other as we never have before, and thereby learning more and more of God's glory.

Just as the New Testament sees 'worship' as something that includes our 'service' to others, as well as the more direct offering of thanks and adoration to God, so it seems reasonable to think that our worship will include seeing His glory through learning what He has done in and for each of us – how He's saved us, rescued us, transformed us throughout our lives. I love having dinner with friends where throughout the meal we swap good stories; millions of years won't be enough to hear each believer's unique story of how the Lord worked – secretly and openly – His symphony of transfiguration in their life. And that will send us back to the throne of God in adoration. The eternal heavenly community is going to be a great place to be!

(An even wilder speculation: maybe that's why Jesus made that odd comment that there's no marriage in heaven, in Matthew 22:30? He can't have meant that we lose the deep closeness we had on earth – it's hard to imagine Him saying, 'Sorry, we don't allow that here!' Maybe the alternative is that *all* relationships we have there are lifted to the maximum, like the best possible marriage... God's infinite love flowing continually through, and so from and to, each member of His Body, world without end?)

And, according to Paul, we shall have bodies: 'redeemed' bodies (Romans 8:23), bodies transformed 'so that they will be like [Christ's] glorious body' (Philippians 3:21); yet still glorious *bodies*. Jesus made a deliberate point of demonstrating in His glorified body that He still enjoyed eating (Luke 24:41)! This bizarre fact can preserve us from any ideas of heaven as something tediously bloodless and passionless. Jesus came to bring us 'life ... to the full' (John 10:10). In heaven we shan't be drifting around as insubstantial ghosts; rather we shall experience the life we were created for (see 2 Corinthians 5:5), for the very first time.

God cares about our bodies. We're made for something richer, something fuller, than what we have now; but what is 'mortal' in us won't be 'unclothed', says Paul, it will 'be swallowed up by life' (2 Corinthians 5:4). The wonderful verses of 1 Corinthians 15:37-44 (please pause to read them!) show us more: our new bodies ('raised in glory … raised in power') may be as unimaginably different from what we have now ('sown in dishonour … sown in weakness') as is the butterfly from the chrysalis it has cast off, or the full-grown wheat from the shrivelled seed we plant. Yet, like the wheat's relation to the seed, they will still be *us*. Perhaps our first steps will be like the first moments after a long illness or injury – that strange feeling of flexing our limbs, gingerly, then more easily, remembering with surprise what it used to feel like to be healthy, without weakness or pain. So probably after death, or Christ's return (Philippians 3:20-21), we shall stretch out in surprise and know, for the first time, what it means to be fully human, fully, gloriously whole.

And Hebrews 10:34 tells us there will be rewards for us, 'better and lasting possessions'. ('Treasures in heaven' as Matthew 6:20 puts it; the 'true riches' Jesus mentions in Luke 16:11.) Even the gift of a cup of cold water back in our past will not go forgotten or unrewarded (Matthew 10:42); our loving God is very good at this! To quote the astonishing words of 1 Corinthians 4:5, 'Each will receive his praise from God'! (Hadn't we assumed it would always be the other way round?!)

But surely heaven will be forward-looking even more than backward-looking. There will be immensely worthwhile things for us to do. Work on earth only became drudgery after the Fall (Genesis 3:17), because of our wilful independence from God. Paul's reference to judging angels (1 Corinthians 6:3) – and probably Jesus' parable about looking after ten cities (Luke 19:17), and His remark about the Master putting His faithful servant 'in charge of all his possessions' (Matthew 24:47) – hint at creative activity in the new heaven and new earth where we'll have many opportunities to build something outrageously, joyfully wonderful to the eternal glory of God.

And all that is just part of the real big picture. Heaven is not only about our individual salvation and transformation, though it certainly is about that. No: heaven is also about the fulfilment of God's master-plan for a whole transfigured cosmos. Romans makes this clear. The first five chapters of Romans set out how we can be forgiven and right with God, warning us against the age-old 'religious' temptation that creates slavery rather than relationship, of trying to please God by our good deeds, our law-keeping or our religious rituals. They climax in the famous verse of Romans 5:1: 'Therefore, since we have been justified through *faith*, we have peace with God through our Lord Jesus Christ' (emphasis mine).

But many Christians act as if Paul stops there, whereas in fact this is just the vital foundation, the removal of the barrier separating us from the great things that follow. Romans 6 announces our transformation, declaring, amazingly: 'Sin shall not be your master' (v14). In other words, there is absolutely no wrongful or destructive behaviour that we cannot break free from, as people whose old innermost self is dead, who are 'born again' and hence 'controlled' now in their deepest being by the Holy Spirit Himself! Chapters 6, 7 and the first half of 8 lead us through how, eventually, that works. *But* there are still greater things to come. What these chapters lead up to is, first, Romans 8:19-21:

> The *creation* waits in eager expectation for the sons of God to be revealed. For the creation was subjected to frustration, not by its own choice, but by the will of the one who subjected it, in hope that the creation itself will be liberated from its bondage to decay and brought into the glorious freedom of the children of God.
>
> (Emphasis mine)[5]

The point here is massive *cosmic* transformation. Here on earth we live in a world where everything decays. But heaven is different. Imagine instead a universe where 'grace reigns' (Romans 5:21): grace, the principle of heaven, God's endless loving creativity forever bringing something out of nothing, from glory to glory. Imagine a universe where all this world's decay and futility have been reversed forever by the glory that has its bridgehead now, invisibly, in God's people; where this world and our entire cosmos 'will be liberated from its bondage to decay'. ('I consider that our present sufferings are not worth comparing with the glory that will be revealed in us', declares Paul three verses earlier [8:18].) It will be a 'new heaven and new earth' where the deterministic, entropic laws of this fallen world – everything gradually

142

disintegrating, falling apart (look at 1 Peter 1:23-25 and Ecclesiastes 1), no beauty that doesn't fade, no achievement that doesn't crumble, no glory that can ultimately endure – are replaced entirely by the loving purposefulness and creativity of God. And there will be 'no more death or mourning or crying or pain, for the old order of things has passed away' (Revelation 21:4).

This is what heaven's about! It is with this cosmic transfiguration that God's long-term purposes begin. (And once again, we can't imagine all the radical change and glory it implies [look at 1 Corinthians 2:9].) Our individual heavenly destinies find their wonderful place within that. Heaven is not some mere epilogue to our life here; rather, our lives here are just the brief preface to the millions of years of joyful wonder to come. And yes, God is doing something crucial with us here, because there are vital lessons we can only learn, vital training we can only experience, in a fallen world where there's suffering and where God sometimes seems absent. And during all that time we are the bridgehead through which the heavenly dimension, the kingdom of God, has been breaking in (Romans 8:21), because in us there is always the seed of the Word, the seed of the alternative universe (1 Peter 1:23; James 1:18). But with the millions of years of eternity, the alternative takes over altogether, and stretches away into distances of glory beyond which our limited imaginations cannot hope to follow. All this is what heaven is about. Now the real game begins.

And even more thrilling and mind-stretching, we shall be just like Jesus! Not merely 'nice'; not even merely holy; but actually 'conformed to the likeness of his Son', with absolutely everything that implies (Romans 8:29). This is the other crucial verse that all the previous parts of Romans have led up to: the goal of all God's loving purposes and planning, the consummation of our entire existence. Or as Galatians wonderfully puts it: Christ will finally have been 'formed in us' (4:19)! Not that we will be clones; God is infinitely creative, and undoubtedly we will each be like Jesus in uniquely diverse and individual ways, true to the glorious personality He has been moulding in each of us. The long, predestined process whereby God has sculptured us, in all we learn and all we suffer, in each act of service, each relationship, each deliberate choice for holiness, each Bible passage or sermon or group study absorbed... God will have woven all this together with unimaginable skill, so that in the end, as we see Jesus completely, we are finally made just like Him (look at 1 John 3:2). All the love, joy, gentleness and power for good of Christ will now be flooding out through us, just as they do through Him. We'll be ready to share Christ's throne (Revelation 3:21; Romans 8:17,32), to share everything that our heavenly Bridegroom is and owns, because heaven will finally have spread right through our personalities. *Thank You, Lord!*

Now we see the point of that odd preposition in Romans 8:18, where Paul spoke of the 'glory that will be revealed *in* us' (emphasis mine), not *to* us; 'that you might share in the glory of our Lord Jesus Christ' (2 Thessalonians 2:14); so that, bizarrely, Jesus might be the 'firstborn among many brothers' (Romans 8:29). (Is that one of those verses where we feel, 'Had I written the Bible I would never have said that'?) But what deeper glory – by definition – could the

Father possibly grant us than to be 'conformed', totally, 'to the likeness of his Son'? 'Attaining to the *whole* measure of the fulness of Christ' (Ephesians 4:13, emphasis mine) – being 'filled to the measure of *all* the fulness of God' (Ephesians 3:19, emphasis mine): these promises, once we really reflect on their meaning, become astonishing. And yet God has predestined nothing less for our futures. 'He who did not spare his own Son, but gave him up for us all – how will he not also, along with him, graciously give us all things?' (Romans 8:32). 'Those he justified, he also glorified'(Romans 8:30): God is a God who delights to share all His glory with us, from top to bottom. Millions of years will never be enough to exhaust it. As Ephesians 3:20 says, what God has planned for us is simply far more than we can ask or imagine.

I love this passage from C S Lewis' *Screwtape Proposes a Toast:*

> There are no ordinary people. You have never talked to a mere mortal. Nations, cultures, arts, civilisations – these are mortal, and their life is to ours as the life of a gnat. But it is immortals whom we joke with, work with, marry, snub, and exploit – immortal horrors or everlasting splendours … It is a serious thing to live in a society of possible gods and goddesses, to remember that the dullest and most uninteresting person you can talk to may one day be a creature which, if you saw it now, you would be strongly tempted to worship, or else a horror and a corruption such as you now meet, if at all, only in a nightmare. All day long we are, in some

degree, helping each other to one or other of these destinations.[6]

'Strongly tempted to worship', because we will be so like Jesus! It's happening already, Paul tells us: 'We ... are being transformed into his likeness with ever-increasing glory, which comes from the Lord, who is the Spirit' (2 Corinthians 3:18).[7] There, at last, it will be complete.

And most joyful of all: we will see Jesus face to face and be with Him forever, the Bride with the Bridegroom at last. 'One thing I ask of the LORD,' David wrote, 'this is what I seek: that I may dwell in the house of the LORD all the days of my life, to gaze upon the beauty of the LORD and to seek him in his temple' (Psalm 27:4). That longing will be totally fulfilled! No: millions of future years will surely not be enough to exhaust all this wonder, glory and joy of heaven! *Thank You, Lord!*

'Millions of years...' – but in heaven there won't be such a thing as time?

Who knows? The eternal world is probably different from this one in endless ways we can't begin to conceive, and here's one last example.[8] But anyway, what can this question mean? We can't imagine heaven as like a block of ice, frozen in motionless perfection forever. We haven't a clue what the possibilities may be, nor how our radically transformed eternal consciousnesses may experience time. Maybe the end of 'time as we know it' means its replacement by some other, heavenly kind of process? Passages like Jesus' parable of the talents hint that we'll have joyful, creative work to do in the new heaven and earth, as we've seen. And the glory of God is infinite, so there's no way we as finite beings can apprehend it all at once – we can't have the capacity for everything God in His love will want to reveal to us and share with us. So does that suggest we'll be involved in an eternal process of continually learning, feeding on, drinking in, more of God – more and more and more? And maybe, where now time is our master and we are its slaves, maybe the heavenly equivalent of time will be a more flexible medium that we can master and sail through in whatever way best enables our growing discovery of God (a day as 1,000 years when it's useful, or 1,000 years as a day)? Who knows! But whatever it is, C S Lewis surely has it right: always 'farther up and farther in' to the glory of God...[9]

Possibilities, interpretations, speculations. Some of them probably completely wrong. Heaven is 'more than we can ask or think'! But we can at least try to imagine what something 'more than we can ask or think' might be like – to think and dream about what it is that no eye has seen, no ear heard – that God has got stored up for those who love Him... That's a huge reason for not letting anyone we care about miss out on all this, because it's only if we've invited heaven in now that we'll have heaven then. But for our own sakes too, as Jesus tells us, we should surely rejoice over what we know about heaven (Luke 10:20)!

So let's reflect thankfully on heaven, dream about how it can be. It has been enormously refreshing preparing this chapter! God wants us to start to grasp, be thrilled, even be awed by, the future He has stored up for us (Ephesians 1:18; Colossians 3:1-2). Let that glory sink deep into your soul, because as we feed on it, we will begin to live it, and it will keep us anchored, helmeted, unbrainwashed, radically and actively devoted, while we're waiting...

We are called to walk the way of Christ's cross in this world, because the cross leads to the resurrection, and beyond that to glory beyond our wildest dreams...

Notes

[1] Sometimes our more sceptical friends ask who these rebels could possibly be. One response is that they can be descendants of godly people, perhaps especially Jews, who repented and lived through the final crisis and entered the millennium. Or, again, children of unbelievers who were themselves not judged and did not perish along with their parents when Christ returned. There are various possibilities. The main point is that our race's this-worldly story ends as it began, with a basic lesson about being human: even in an earthly paradise we can so easily rebel against God.

[2] The Evangelical Alliance has produced a very helpful study of this issue titled *The Nature of Hell* (2000).

[3] In fact 'heavenly realms' is better translated here and elsewhere (see Ephesians 6:12) as 'the supernatural realms'. In this chapter, however, we're using the word 'heaven' in its conventional sense for the realm 'in Christ' in which we shall live out our glorious future eternal life.

[4] D A Carson, *Expositor's Bible Commentary on Matthew* (Zondervan, 1995), p461. Watchman Nee comments on the words of Revelation 20:11 'Earth and sky fled … and there was no place for them': 'Some consider this fleeing of the earth and heaven as only a divine act of re-making, but the succeeding clause, "and there was found no place for them" [AV], clearly shows that the old heaven and earth are completely destroyed'. *Come, Lord Jesus* (Christian Fellowship Publishers, 1976), p221.

[5] For a more in–depth treatment of these exceptionally glorious chapters see Pete Lowman, *Gateways to God: Seeking Spiritual Depth in a Post-Modern World* (Christian Focus, 2001), chapter 6.

[6] C S Lewis, *Screwtape Proposes a Toast* (Collins, 1965), p109. © copyright CS Lewis Pte Ltd 1959. Quoted by permission.

[7] Interestingly, and practically, this key passage about the means of our transformation is actually talking about reading God's Word the Bible (see the context from v14). Peter likewise focuses on the Word of God as the imperishable seed of our new life in 1 Peter 1:23-25.

[8] This whole aspect, incidentally, is something that (going back to the question of the rapture) LaHaye for example forgets when he mocks the 'post-trib' view that Christ's people will meet Him in the air as He descends from heaven and then return to earth with Him: 'We zip up to the Father's house, take a quick peek in there, and zip right back down moments later with Christ ... The post-Trib theory allows no time for the Judgment Seat of Christ [cf 2 Corinthians 5:10] and the Marriage Supper of the Lamb [Revelation 19] ... Only the pre-Trib position allows sufficient time (at least seven years) for these events to be fulfilled with dignity and grace' (*The Rapture*, pp123-24). It's strange that LaHaye can't see how an extended period of 'heaven-time' fully sufficient for these might yet appear only momentary in earth's time. And as for the marriage supper, again LaHaye doesn't allow for the possibility that our transformed consciousnesses might function simultaneously in both the earthly dimension and the heavenly dimension of the marriage supper too. After all, Ephesians 2:6 makes clear that we live in the heavenly dimension as well as the earthly one even now; we just aren't conscious of it. And in the eternal state we may well be transformed in all kinds of other, unimaginable ways!

[9] C S Lewis, *The Last Battle* (Collins, 1980) p211. © copyright CS Lewis Pte Ltd 1956. Quoted by permission.

Appendix A

Matthew 24: What Does Jesus Say About His Return?

Matthew 24 is arguably the single most significant Bible chapter on the end times, and Jesus' most sustained teaching on the subject. Yet it's not entirely easy to interpret. Then again, we can hardly say to the Lord that we're going to write off His sustained teaching in this chapter because it's too difficult! So this appendix sets out some options.

Let's start with two problems. First: At the start of the chapter the disciples ask Jesus two questions (v3). One is following up His statement in verse 2 that the magnificent Jewish temple will be completely demolished: 'When will that happen?' The other is, 'What will be the sign of your coming and of the end of the age?'

When we look at Jesus' reply, we find that parts of it seem very relevant to AD70 when the Romans destroyed that temple (particularly when we look at Luke 21's record of the same discourse). However, other parts clearly seem to speak to the second question – Matthew 24:14, for example, or 24:30 where Jesus describes 'the Son of Man coming on the clouds of the sky, with power and great glory'. But whereas the disciples – who perhaps couldn't conceive of the temple's destruction without it being also the 'end of the age' – were comfortable putting these two questions together, we know that AD70 has already proved to be separated by nearly 2,000 years from Jesus' coming in glory. So how do we know when Jesus is responding to one or the other of these questions? How do we know which verses to use in building our understanding of Christ's 'coming and the end of the age'?

And then there's a second problem. In verse 34 we find Jesus saying that 'this generation will certainly not pass away until all these things have happened'. *All* of them? Both the temple's destruction *and* the second coming?

Liberal scholars often look at that and argue that Jesus is predicting the events leading up to the fall of Jerusalem in verses 8-24 as belonging with the End and His second coming ('immediately after the distress of those days') in verses 29-31, and finishing 'this generation will certainly not pass away until *all* these things have happened' (v34, emphasis mine); and they conclude that He was simply wrong. 'Generation' in verse 34 means forty years or so, they say, and everything in the chapter before this was supposed to happen within that time; Jesus thought the End was near, and He was mistaken. (C S Lewis' 'The World's Last Night' sees v34 as the 'most embarrassing verse in the Bible', while observing that the fact that it's recorded at all says a lot for the Gospels' reliability – and also how interesting it is that this problematic verse comes right before Jesus' statement that He [by choice!] *doesn't* know when the End will come [v36].)[1]

But there are several facts that the liberal approach doesn't allow for. First, of course, we must then go the whole hog and say, if Jesus was entirely wrong about this vital matter, His teaching is not reliable, and it is hard to know when or why He should be trusted about anything else. (Particularly since it is precisely here that He emphasises the trustworthiness of His teaching [v35].) An Old Testament prophet was to be executed if His predictions didn't come true: how, since Jesus' predictions don't come true, is He a true prophet from God? (And of course He claims far more than that.) But then a host of data kicks in to remind us that we are on the wrong track here, because there are such good reasons for believing that Jesus really was God.

But let's stick to the evidence in this chapter itself. It's odd, if Jesus is saying 'The End is soon', that the thrust of His teaching in Matthew 24:4,6 (see especially the phrasing Luke records in Luke 21:8-9), and in Matthew 24:48 and 25:5,19, is to cool down expectation, not to heat it up; He is preparing them for a longish (at least) absence on His part. In contrast, He says in Luke 21:8, those who say, 'The time is near,' are *false* prophets.

Most importantly, however, the early Church evidently weren't embarrassed by this verse. If many of the liberals were right and the Gospels were written after AD70 (ie a 'generation' after Jesus), then surely the Gospel writers would have edited out so damaging a saying – *if* it really meant that the End would come within forty years; but Matthew, Mark and Luke all left it in. Or we can come at it from the other end: the writers of the Gospels clearly thought Jesus was God incarnate, so *they* could not have thought He would have said something so utterly mistaken as that the End of history would certainly come within forty years: hence, whatever these words meant for them, this cannot be it.

And indeed there are other things this word 'generation' (v34) can mean that resolve the problem. If we check some of Jesus' other uses of the word, we see He also uses it to mean 'group or type of people' (eg Matthew 11:16 and 17:17). And that's how it's sometimes used elsewhere in the Bible, eg in the Greek Septuagint translation of Psalm 24:6; or in the ESV of Psalm 12:7 (where the NIV has 'such people') and 14:5 (again see the ESV).

This opens up several alternative possibilities:

1. Chrysostom and others have seen 'this generation' as meaning 'this group of people' and referring to His disciples. In that case, in Matthew 24:34 Jesus is stating, by way of encouragement, the remarkable fact that despite all the terrible events He has just prophesied in verses 21-22, His followers (particularly in Judaea, vv15-16) will make it through. Christ's words will not pass away (v35), so nor will the people of the Word; indeed, this was why those days were 'shortened' (v22). Jesus is then giving a promise but also a challenge (see also 24:13 and Luke 21:36): amazingly, the persecution will be overcome, Jesus' true disciples will survive; will you be one of them?

However, the negative usage of 'generation' in Luke 17:25, which is in some ways a parallel passage, might make this less likely.[2]

2. In referring to 'this group of people', He could be speaking of the Jewish race. (Ryle, Hendriksen and, much earlier, Jerome have seen it this way, and the NIV offers

'race' as an alternative reading in the margin.) It is remarkable that as a race the Jews (unlike, say, the Moabites or the Ammonites or the Edomites) have survived all that history has thrown at them, including Jerusalem's destruction, with their identity intact. This says something to the glory of God – see Paul's remarks in Romans 11 on God's ongoing and (Romans 9:6) undefeated purposes for the Jews, which lead him towards the cry of praise in 11:33. However, to me at least, it is difficult to see the point Jesus is making here, if the Jewish race as a whole is what is meant.

3. A better option is that He is referring to the Jewish unbelievers who, amazingly, will go on rejecting Him. William Kelly wrote many years ago:

> He is saying, as it were, I will prepare you for the terrible truth [cf Romans 9:3], that this Christ-rejecting generation is to continue till all these things are fulfilled … It might have been supposed that while Christianity was going over the whole earth, and making conquests everywhere, if one nation more than another was to be brought under the power of Christ, it must be Israel, loved for the fathers' sakes. But no.[3]

Better education, for example, will not alter this. And Christ may also be saying that they will go on catastrophically disbelieving even as the signs of the end accumulate around them. This makes particular sense if an aspect of the final crisis-period is God speaking in a fresh way to the ethnic Jews.

Mark 8:12 might be a helpful parallel here, where 'generation' may well refer, not to a particular age-group, but to the unbelieving type of people who are demanding a sign, because they were ignoring the sign the believers had just been given (8:8-9). This also seems to be the meaning of 'unbelieving generation' in Mark 9:19 (rather than a forty-year age-group), and as we've noted in the Septuagint Greek of Psalm 12:7 (see ESV).

It is even possible on this understanding that Matthew 24:34 starts a new paragraph of Jesus' discourse, saying that this 'generation', the type of people described in verse 38, will not pass away until disaster comes; Jesus' words won't pass away – they'll indeed be fulfilled – but no one knows when the End will actually come, and so this wretched kind of people, heedless and foolish, will carry on just as they are until catastrophe comes upon them.[4] The flow of thought there is attractive.

Verse 34, then, is not as problematic as it first appears, and doesn't determine how we read this chapter. But we still have to deal with the fact that in this chapter Jesus is answering two questions from verses 2-3: one about when the destruction of the magnificent Jewish temple would happen, which followed in AD70; and the other about the sign of His coming and of the end of the age, which would seem to point to the End of history and to verses 27-31 at least. How do we recognise when He is talking about one or the other? Here are the three most obvious possibilities.

Option one: It's all in the future

One way to read Jesus' discourse is as being almost entirely about the end-times; from the clear reference to 'the end' in v14, through the unique 'distress' of v15-28, to, 'immediately after' this (v29), 'at that time' (v30), the second coming. This makes completely coherent sense of Matthew 24 as a whole.

But there is a big problem with this approach: it doesn't fit what is usually seen as the meaning of the parallel chapter in Luke: Luke 21. The verses about the attack on Jerusalem in Luke 21:20-24 are usually seen as being about AD70, after which 'Jerusalem will be trampled on by the Gentiles until the times of the Gentiles are fulfilled'. Only after this does Luke move on to record Jesus' teaching about the end times.

That is not an insuperable obstacle. We could read these verses, and hence Luke 21 as a whole, as referring to the end time too. Instead of referring to the dispersion of the Jews after AD70, verses 23-24 could be predicting the beginning of an end-time destruction of the entire state of Israel of the kind demanded by Iranian president Ahmadinejad (it is 'When the power of the holy people has been finally broken' that the End comes, Daniel 12:7), accompanied by the mass deportation of many Israelis to other countries. There is a difficulty, however. The Matthew equivalent, 24:15-21, seems (as we've seen in an earlier chapter) to be describing the same events as Daniel 9:27 and 12:7,11, and 2 Thessalonians 2:3-4; and the most obvious way of reading these is that the 'setting up of the abomination of desolation' in the temple by the invading end-time satanic dictator happens at, and marks, the *start*

157

of 1,260 days of terror. But if the Jews being deported en masse in Luke 21:24 refers to that moment, how is it (besides demonic seduction, Revelation 16:14) that 'all the nations' are gathered together again to fight 'against Jerusalem' at the *end* of that time, immediately before the second coming in Zechariah 12 and 14?

But there is a further major objection to any approach that sees these chapters in all three Gospels as being entirely about the end time: if that's so, the question about the first-century temple's destruction, which alone triggers the entire discourse in both Mark's and Luke's accounts, was never answered at all by Jesus. And as He speaks of Jerusalem's destruction, He does not even hint that what He describes is far removed in time from the destruction they have specifically asked about. That seems very strange indeed.

Option two: It's mostly in the past

A second possibility has been advocated by an increasing number of evangelical writers, who see the bulk of the chapter, right through to Matthew 24:35, as Jesus' teaching about AD70, answering the disciples' question about when the temple will be destroyed, and explaining en route that, terrible as those events within the next generation will be, they should not see them as the end times (compare v6). This creates a straightforward parallel with the usual view of Luke 21 as being about AD70, at least up to 21:24; it makes complete sense of Matthew 24:34; and it also explains the sudden shift from the certainties of Matthew 24:32-34 to the uncertainty of verses 36,42-44, because these latter verses are where Jesus turns to answer the disciples' questions about 'your coming and ... the end of the age'.[5]

There are obvious issues here with making verses 29-31 describe events around AD70. But both R T France and Tom Wright read verse 29, which describes the sun being darkened and the stars falling from the sky 'immediately' after the terrible events of AD70, as a typical apocalyptic way of describing the (admittedly earth-shattering) political and religious convulsions when Jerusalem is destroyed.[6] (Compare the non-literal imagery in Psalm 18:7,14-15, a situation where David's history is an example of an apocalyptic pattern; also Judges 5:4-5, Isaiah 13:10 on the fall of Babylon [a verse which is being alluded to here], Ezekiel 32:7-9 on the destruction of Egypt, and Amos 8:9-10 or Micah 1:4-5 on the fall of Samaria.[7])

Then, *secondly*, they both take Christ's 'coming with power and great glory ... at that time' in verse 30 as being His coming to the Father in the ascension as described in Daniel 7:13-14, not His coming back in glory to this world; while His vindication on earth is consummated by the events of AD70. (These approaches do obviously help with the problematic Matthew 24:34, because there 'all these things' seems to include the coming of the Son of Man, but now that can be understood as first-century.)

A similar explanation was presented by the great Alfred Edersheim in the nineteenth century, where 'coming' in Matthew 24:30, like Matthew 21:40-41, refers to Christ's coming to Israel in vindication and judgement in AD70. ('It is scarcely conceivable', Edersheim suggests, 'that these sayings would have been allowed to stand' [at least without interpretative comment?], unless the early Church had understood them as being about AD70, and as answering the first question in verses 2-3.[8])

And then, *thirdly*, these writers view verse 31, the 'gathering of the elect' by the angels (or 'messengers'), as referring to the preaching of the gospel, newly motivated now that Israel is so clearly not the centre of God's plan.

But there are a whole series of problems with this approach:

1. Firstly, we might well feel that the simplest way to read Matthew 24:15ff is following straight on from verse 14, where Jesus is already talking about the End when the gospel has been preached to all nations. Admittedly it's possible that having described in verse 14 the most important marker of the ultimate End, He then returns in verse 15 onwards to give very practical advice about their other question, regarding the destruction of Jerusalem's temple in AD70. But it's still difficult to see these next verses as being about AD70. Don Carson makes the point that in AD70, by the time the Romans had actually desecrated the temple, it was far too late for anyone to flee in the way verse 16 exhorts.[9] F F Bruce points out that in AD70 the desecrating sacrilege didn't happen in the holy place (compare v15) but in the temple court;[10] and 'non-literalist' Storms has to admit that none of the events of AD70 'quite fits what this verse says'.[11]

We should note, too, that Luke (17:31) records Jesus teaching the dire warning of the next verses, Matthew 24:17-18, in the same context ('that night', Luke 17:34-35) as the verses Matthew records in 24:39-41 about the 'coming of the Son of Man', which France himself agrees are about the end times (just as Luke 17:24 and Luke 18:8 also in the same context would seem to be). And then, the Daniel passages to which Jesus (or Matthew; either way, God) links the desecration of the temple in verse 15 would seem to be Daniel 9:27 and 12:9-11, and both of these seem clearly to refer to the end time.[12] So, most certainly, does 2 Thessalonians 2:1-8, where Paul likewise presents the desecration of the temple as the key sign that the end-time climax of history has come. All this seems to be strong evidence for reading these verses in Matthew 24:15ff as being about the end times.

2. But that's not all. Surely the emphasis on the unique horror of the days of Matthew 24:21-22 ('There will be great distress, unequalled from the beginning of the world until now – and never to be equalled again. If those days had not been cut short, no-one would survive') makes it very hard to see this part of Matthew 24 as limited to – or even primarily about – Palestine in AD70. Indeed, they match Daniel 12:1 ('a time of distress such as has not happened from the beginning of nations until then'), which is very clearly about 'the time of the end' (look at Daniel 12:2-4). Riddlebarger rightly comments:

> The events of the fall of Jerusalem ... simply are not the worst tribulation that men have brought or experienced on the earth.[13]

Given Jesus' statement that the whole of human history will contain nothing worse, were the events of AD70 really worse than the holocaust? (Or, in terms of loss of life, the flood?)

3. Then moving on, please look again at Matthew 24:29-31, because these verses present a whole range of further

problems for this view. What political event around AD70 is the supposedly apocalyptic language of stars falling in verse 29 referring to, since it happens 'immediately *after'* (emphasis mine) the uniquely horrific time of verses 21-22? Clearly not the ruining of the temple, because that has already happened at the beginning of that terrible time in verse 15. Indeed, it seems strange if Jesus is speaking about the events of AD70 here but in an apocalyptic way, given that Luke 21:20 records Him speaking of them entirely prosaically in the very same discourse. In fact, the parallel verses to Matthew 24:29-31 in Luke 21:25-27 ('Men will faint from terror ... for the heavenly bodies will be shaken') sound like something even bigger than the fall of Jerusalem; they sound like literal (and terrifying) 'signs in the sky' visible to everyone (cf Matthew 24:30), rather than mere metaphors for the fall of Jerusalem. Again the end times seem to be in view. (We might note too that when Revelation 6:12-13 uses almost the same words, it is clearly talking about the end times [see 6:15-17].)

4. Then, next, as regards Christ's 'coming' in Matthew 24:30, if this verse is about a cosmic 'coming to the Father' by Jesus (as in Daniel 7:13), not Christ's end-time coming to the earth in glory, then presumably Matthew 24:27 ('For as lightning that comes from the east is visible even in the west, so will be the coming of the Son of Man') is not about His coming back to this earth either. But then whatever is Jesus' point in that verse? And surely 'in the sky' (v30) makes most sense as being in the time of the second coming. And clearly the nations who are *on the earth* ... apprehensive of what is coming on the world' (emphasis mine) are the 'they' who see Christ coming in 'great glory'

(Luke 21:25-27), not any cosmic audience to the events of Daniel 7:13. Looking at Matthew 24:26-27,37,39,42-44 and 50, it is hard not to feel that when Jesus refers to His 'coming' He most consistently means His return openly to *this* world. (Likewise if we turn to Matthew 16:27, 23:39, or 26:64, or indeed John 14:3.)

In particular, what Matthew 25:31-32 in this same discourse says about Christ's coming 'in his glory' (compare 24:30 'coming with power and great glory') is very clearly about the end times and His return to *this* world:

> 'When the Son of Man comes in his glory … he
> will sit on his throne in heavenly glory. All the
> nations will be gathered before him, and he will
> separate the people one from another as a
> shepherd separates the sheep from the goats.'

If, on the other hand, we want to think of 24:30 as being about Christ coming to Jerusalem in AD70 *invisibly* in judgement, it is hard to fit this with 'They will *see* the Son of Man' (emphasis mine). The same is true of verse 27, since it was certainly not so blindingly obvious to the unbelieving Jews in AD70 that Christ's 'coming' was what was happening then.[14] Nor does Christ's invisible vindication through the events of AD70 seem the most obvious thing for the disciples to have meant when they spoke of 'your coming' in their question of verse 2 (following as it does on 23:38). Douglas Moo, at least, is willing to state clearly that in the New Testament in general Jesus' 'coming on the clouds' 'always has reference to the Parousia' (Jesus' coming back to earth at the End).[15]

Again, Luke 17 records Jesus giving much of the same teaching as in Matthew 24, but when He moves on to 'when the Son of Man comes', the question is 'will he find faith *on the earth?*' (Luke 18:8, emphasis mine).

A further issue is that Luke's parallel to Matthew 24:30 about Jesus' 'coming' is Luke 21:27, and the point Luke records Jesus as making in all this is, 'When these things begin to take place, stand up and lift up your heads, because your redemption is drawing near ... when you see these things happening, you know that the kingdom of God is near' (Luke 21:28-31, the parallel to Matthew 24:32-33). It's exceptionally hard to understand these verses if 'these things' is about the horrors of AD70. How could this tragedy and its central 'abomination' be reasons for joyful 'lifting up your heads' for any believer who was a Jew? (Compare Paul's attitude to the Jerusalem temple in Acts 21:26.) How was the bloodshed that accompanied the AD70 fall of Jerusalem a pointer that 'the kingdom of God is near' (Luke 21:31), in the same imminent sense that summer is soon to follow when the fig leaves come out (v29); what happened *after* AD70 that this could possibly be referring to? Or, to apply the question to the end of Luke 21:28, what 'redemption' followed AD70? The obvious conclusion seems to be that Luke 21:27-28, and therefore their parallel in Matthew 24:30, refer rather to the 'redemption' (compare Ephesians 1:14, 4:30) that happens at Christ's second coming in glory.[16]

5. Moving on lastly to Matthew 24:31, those who see the whole chapter as being about AD70 have to see the 'angels' (or 'messengers') who are sent 'with a loud trumpet call ... [to] gather his elect' as the missionaries preaching the

gospel worldwide as the first century continued. But would anybody read this as something so mundane after the preceding two verses if it were not for other considerations? It certainly seems that references elsewhere to the angels in connection with Christ's coming, in Matthew 13:41 (especially), 16:27 and 25:31, all have to do with supernatural beings, and with the End; not with AD70, nor with missionaries. We must also ask, just how did AD70 make any difference to the spread of the gospel?[17] World evangelism proceeds very fruitfully throughout Acts, long before the temple falls.[18]

All in all, then, interpretations seeing Matthew 24:4-35 as entirely about the fall of Jerusalem in the first century don't really fit the text. Most of it – particularly verses 14, 21-22 and 29-31 – makes most sense when seen as describing the End.[19]

(And incidentally, all this has a practical significance: people – or a church – are much more likely to take the trouble to dig into this passage that Matthew gave so much space to, *if* indeed we have good reasons to hope it will teach us about the end-times that we may possibly live through, rather than about the long-passed events of AD70!)

Option three: Double fulfilment

If, then, we can't see the chapter as limited either entirely to the end times or entirely to AD70, we have to take on board the idea that these prophecies have some sort of double fulfilment, in both eras. (Or to quote Cranfield's respected commentary on Mark:

> It seems then that neither an exclusively historical nor an exclusively eschatological interpretation is satisfactory, and that we must allow for a double reference, for a mingling of historical and eschatological.[20])

Whether we like it or not, God the master Artist has a way of shaping history where earlier events foreshadow or even somehow participate in the ultimate events of the End.

Scholars often speak of 'prophetic foreshadowing' in Old Testament prophecies to describe the way they set together predictions of a suffering and reigning Messiah, or combine Christ's first and second comings, even though the fulfilments of these were widely separated in time. (See, for example, Zechariah 9:9-10, or Isaiah 53;[21] or the well-known example of Isaiah 61:2 – when Jesus quotes this passage in Luke 4:19 He omits the part about the day of vengeance and judgement, that being for a later time.)

This phenomenon is often illustrated from the way mountain peaks that are actually far apart can seem to be close together if seen from a distance;[22] it is only as we draw nearer that we realise the true distance between them. So is it not with this same 'prophetic foreshadowing' that Jesus answers both of the disciples' questions in Matthew 24:3 together, combining His responses to the question about the destruction of Jerusalem and its temple (which happened in AD70), with their other question, 'What will be the sign of your coming and of the end of the age?'?

So as we compare Matthew's record of Jesus' discourse, which makes almost complete sense viewed as speaking entirely about the End, with Luke 21:5-24, which makes most sense seen as speaking about AD70, we may well ask whether history under God's hand has something of a spiral nature; whether a pattern was partially embodied in the events of AD70 that will develop in its final form at the end of the age. Indeed, we might even wonder if at the time of the Olivet discourse it was not yet certain that these two would be separate. It seems that if the Jews (or a large minority, at least) had accepted God's clear offer in Acts 3:19-21 of repenting so 'that times of refreshing may come from the Lord, and that he may send the Christ ... He must remain in heaven until the time comes for God to restore everything' – then the culminating events of history and the second coming would have happened. And then – to take a parallel from quantum physics – perhaps the 'waveform would have collapsed' (!), the two would have remained one. Until that time, therefore, the split between the two was not yet determined (so inevitably the prophecy would be unclear?). And it might seem from Matthew 24:36 that Christ Himself shared (as in Hebrews 4:15) His contemporaries' pain in not knowing how long it would be before everything was fulfilled, before God stepped in and put everything right.[23]

But to say that it seems that there is a 'spiral' character to history, as divinely shaped, is to say something more: it's to say that sometimes God builds a pattern into history that will finally emerge clearly in the end time, but manifests partially earlier. It may be a very alien thought to our secularised mindset, where human history goes its own sweet way with God's purposes being almost tangential to it. But whether we like it or not, the Old Testament often seems to express this, presenting what is happening at that moment as a God-ordained foreshadowing of the future, and so tying it into the black-and-white revelation of how things are in the ultimate End. Joel 2 is a good example: the apocalyptic language of 2:10 is used to underline the seriousness of a contemporary locust plague (which is only 'like' a mighty human army, 2:5,7); but then, as we watch 2:19 and chapter 3 develop, we find the events of Joel's time merging into a pattern that manifests fully with the judgement on all nations that he foresees taking place in Palestine at the End. And look at Zechariah 3:8: 'Listen, O high priest Joshua and your associates seated before you, who are *men symbolic of things to come* ... ' (emphasis mine).

Another Old Testament parallel would be the 'dual fulfilments' of typology, the way in which contemporary situation and messianic fulfilment merge in and out again in some of the psalms: Psalm 2, for example, or 22; or Psalm 40 (combining vv 6-8 which Hebrews 10 applies to Christ, with the confession of sin in v12); or Psalm 69 (where v9 is messianic, and vv5 and 23 are not). Or, again, the way that Cyrus as impending deliverer of Israel in Isaiah 41:25 merges into the ultimate Messiah in 42:1-4, and back out again in chapter 45.[24] In much of Isaiah, writes Motyer, the prophet

> envisages the ultimate acts of God, though seeing them in thought-forms suggested by the historical crisis through which the people of God are to pass.[25]

It may feel alien to us, but this foreshadowing and dual fulfilment are evidently how God sometimes works in Scripture and in history.

And so it is that the events of the end times that seem to be described in Matthew 24:9-31 (particularly vv14,21-22,29-31), including verse 15, following as it does from the reference to 'the end' of verse 14, and apparently leading straight through to the uniquely horrific 'then' of verse 21, nevertheless seem 'prefigured', paralleled, foreshadowed, by the previous embodiment of the spiral, the previous desecration of Jerusalem, in AD70, which Luke 21:20-24 seem to focus on more clearly. (As that in turn was prefigured, we should note, by what Antiochus Epiphanes did in 168BC, Daniel 11:31.[26])

We may suggest, then, that Jesus' complete answer to the two questions of 24:3 reflected this double fulfilment, and God in His goodness has clarified matters by giving us multiple versions of the Olivet discourse: He used Matthew and Mark to focus more on the second question and set out the end-time fulfilment (which would also apply to AD70 insofar as AD70 was a foreshadowing of that fulfilment); and He inspired Luke to focus rather more on the AD70 events, which is the sole topic of the disciples' question as Luke records it in 21:7. (Although Luke too merges into what is almost certainly the second coming in 21:25-27.[27]) For our purposes in this book, therefore, Matthew 24:15-22 may rightly be read as giving us vital instruction about the climax of history.

Finding the flow

In that case, then, we may read Matthew 24 like this:

1. In verse 3, the disciples pose their two questions. What does Jesus focus His answer on? Verse 4 seems to be the thing they really need to know above all (and compare vv11,23,24), along with the warnings and challenge of verses 9-13 (just as the book of Revelation is given – arguably – to help believers survive the toughest times as 'overcomers').

In verse 6 He seems to be saying, 'The wars are not the point; downplay them as signs.' That doesn't mean, however, that the experience of these things is meaningless. Suffering, in the New Testament, always leads to glory, and these things aren't meaningless; they are the 'beginning of *birth*-pains' (v8, cf Romans 8:22, emphasis mine). There's huge glory to come, although we have to pass through pain along the way. But still the vital thing is not to be deceived, because the 'beginning of birth-pains' is not 'the end' (v6), nor is it the climax of verse 14.[28]

2. Matthew 24:9-13: Jesus' flow of thought seems to be moving on here to a more specific period ('At that time', v10). There is a sense of a time coming when the pressure ramps up. (Presumably we are no longer in the *'beginning* of birth-pains' now [emphasis mine]?) Still the things they should focus on are not external signs but internal challenges, as with verses 23-26. But isn't He already starting to focus on the more apocalyptic times – with AD70 in view, but particularly (v14) the End? 'All nations' in verse 9 also implies that the primary reference of these verses is not AD70.

3. Matthew 24:15-28: Arguably we are now in a new section and must ask when it refers to. Here is where the spiral or 'double fulfilment' understanding is so helpful, because if we look at the parallel section in Luke 21:20-24, we seem to be looking at AD70; but in the version God has given us in Matthew, verses 21 and 22 (which have no equivalent in Luke) describe a period of horror that is emphasised as absolutely unique in world history and must surely belong to the end time (as does Daniel 12:1-2, which uses almost the same words). Verses 21-22 also clearly link this time period (leading on from the abomination of v15, which has to be the 'then' in v21) to the End that is referred to at its beginning in verse 14, and that comes 'immediately' after it according to the verses that directly follow (vv29-31).[29] We can assume, therefore, that these Matthew verses give us instruction about the End (whatever other fulfilment they may have had that is drawn out in Luke's version).

4. Matthew 24:29-31: 'Immediately after the distress of those days' (presumably the same distress as verses 22-23 ['those days'], and therefore of v15), the second coming occurs. The 'sign of the Son of Man ... in the sky' of verse 30 is the true answer to the second question in verse 3, rather than the false signs of verse 6 or verse 24. The key (and thrilling) point here is surely the ultimate cosmic sovereignty of Jesus, even at a time of unequalled evil (v21) – when, as Hendriksen puts it, 'the earth is drenched with the blood of the saints in the most terrible tribulation of all time'.[30]

5. Then comes the problematic section of 24:32-34, which we discussed at the beginning of this Appendix.

Verses 32-33 encourage Christ's disciples to hold firm in faith (v13) through the terrible events described in verses 15-24. Verse 34 is more difficult, and what practically we learn from it will depend on how we understand the word 'generation' in this verse; see the discussion at the start of this Appendix.

6. The next part, 24:36-42, is also difficult, for different reasons, and we discuss it in the Appendix that follows. Verses 36-42 present us with very practical warnings to be alert for the unexpected 'coming of the Son of Man'. This may refer to the rapture, or else possibly to the coming of judgement, particularly on Judaea. (These are quite important verses for the feasibility of the whole 'pre-trib' framework.) But they lead into the closing section, verses 43-51, and the challenges here, at least, are clear, pressing, and practical: see chapter 1 of this study.

We can be confident, then, that although our Lord planned His discourse (and its record in Luke 21 especially) to equip those in Judaea who needed to be readied for the tragic events of AD70, its usefulness certainly did not terminate there. It is for us too, His Church down the ages, that He gave Matthew 24 and its unique revelations about the end time that we must allow to 'teach, correct, rebuke and train' us, so that we may be 'thoroughly equipped for every good work' (2 Timothy 3:17). This chapter is foundational for our understanding of 'your coming and the end of the age'; it's worth the effort!

Notes

1 C S Lewis, *Fern-seed and Elephants* (Collins, 1975), pp69-70.
© copyright CS Lewis Pte Ltd 1975. Quoted by permission.

2 It might also be slightly odd if, by using both 'you' and 'that generation' in verse 34, Jesus is addressing the same people in both the second and third person. But the 'you' could be specific to the four leaders who raised the question, Mark 13:4; cf Mark 13:37.

3 William Kelly, *Notes on Daniel* (G Morrish, 1881), p224.

4 There are numerous other possibilities. Another is that 'these things' in Matthew 24:33 obviously don't include the second coming of verse 30 itself; so conceivably there is a jump of thought here: a jump from AD70 in the preceding verses up to verse 26, into a digression about the second coming in verses 27-31 (a digression to make clear that they should not listen to the false prophets of verse 26, because when Christ indeed returns it will be very obvious), before returning to AD70 and 'this generation' in vv32-35. This works even better with the parallel verses in Luke: Luke 21:32 could be read as coming back to AD70 as described – probably – in verse 24, after a digression about the second coming in, say, verses 25-28. So then the 'these things' of Matthew 24:32-35 refers back particularly to verses 15-26 and AD70. Then, when Jesus has completed that line of thought about 'this generation' in verse 35, He returns in verse 36 to the unforeseeable second coming, ie to 'that day' of verses 27-31. (Variants of this view are proposed by eg Karl Barth [*Church Dogmatics* (T & T Clark, 1960), III/2], C E B Cranfield [*The Gospel According to St Mark* (Cambridge University Press, 1972), p409] and Craig Blomberg [in *Jesus and the Restoration of Israel*, ed Carey Newman, p33].) This is attractive. But the big snag with it is surely the 'immediately after the distress of those days' in v29 ('in those

days', Mark 13:24); which seems to make clear that verse 29 follows directly after the 'distress' of verses 21-22.

[5] R T France, whose Tyndale commentary on Matthew is a good example of the 'mostly in the past' approach, says that when Matthew speaks of the 'end of the age' in verses 36ff, as also in passages like 13:39-41 and 49-50, he does clearly mean the end time. Tom Wright, however, goes a lot further, asserting that the whole of Matthew 24 is about AD70 and none of it (not even vv43-50) is about the second coming; since, strikingly, 'during his earthly ministry, Jesus said nothing about his return' (*Surprised by Hope*, p137) – although (oddly, we might think?) the early Church did. But can this be? (Matthew 16:27? 23:39? 25:31? 26:64? John 14:3?) There is no space here for a full scholarly assessment of the weaknesses in Wright's arguments on this topic; but see the symposium *Jesus and the Restoration of Israel* (ed Carey Newman), particularly the essays by Blomberg and Allison.

[6] Tom Wright says without any qualification that for first-century readers the 'one thing [this verse] didn't mean was something to do with the actual sun, moon and stars in the sky' (*Matthew for Everyone* [SPCK, 2002], p122). But as Stafford Wright points out, 'When Jesus Christ was born, a strange star hung in the sky, and at his crucifixion the sun was blacked out ... Peter probably refers to these heavenly and earthly phenomena when he quotes from Joel in his sermon in Acts 2:19-20. His hearers would have experienced them' (in *Handbook of Biblical Prophecy*, ed Carl Armerding and Ward Gasque, pp170-71).

[7] But there is definitely another way of looking at these poetic images. Rather than being purely illustrative, they may be linking the contemporary political events into a supra-historical pattern that manifests fully in the End – the 'double fulfilment' we shall consider below. Matthew's phrasing here comes firstly

from Isaiah 13:10 about the fall of Babylon; but arguably, with its reference to 'the world' in 13:11-12, that Isaiah passage refocuses on the End. Another source for Matthew's phrasing is Isaiah 34:4, and again, although this chapter focuses on Edom in 34:9ff, 34:2 is about the judgement of 'all nations'.

[8] Alfred Edersheim, *The Life and Times of Jesus the Messiah* (1886; various reprinted editions), III/xxvii.

[9] D A Carson, *Expositor's Bible Commentary on Matthew*, p500.

[10] F F Bruce, *Word Biblical Commentary on 1 and 2 Thessalonians*, p181.

[11] Sam Storms, *Kingdom Come*, p247.

[12] See John Lennox, *Against the Flow*, p304. Storms, pp81-91, tries to make Daniel 9:27 refer to AD70, but it is at the cost of treating Daniel's 70 'sevens' as not having any literal numerical significance, even though Daniel himself seems clearly to have been taking the seventy years at the start of the chapter (v2) entirely literally. (Literal 'sevens' of years were of course very important in Jewish culture, because of the joyous jubilee arrangements of Leviticus 25.) Again, I was amazed at the weakness of the treatment of this section in both Storms and his fellow non-literalist Kim Riddlebarger (*A Case for Amillennialism*, pp181-84): neither even face the (to my mind) fatal problems the chapter's last sentence poses for their attempts to make it apply to Christ (Riddlebarger) or Titus (Storms) in the first century, rather than to the end-time dictator.

[13] Riddlebarger, p307.

[14] Storms, trying hard to fit this verse into AD70, bizarrely reinterprets it as saying that 'The people of Jerusalem will then recognise how they had mistreated their Messiah, but their mourning will not be the sort that comes from heartfelt

repentance but rather a woeful and wailing lamentation that arises from their having witnessed his ultimate vindication and triumph' (p270); that is, that as a result of the catastrophe of AD70, 'all the tribes of the land', all of Israel, 'saw' that Jesus was enthroned in heaven and was now being vindicated against those who had crucified Him. But did they? How can we possibly say that 'all' the unbelieving Jews realised this as a result of AD70?

[15] In *Three Views on the Rapture*, ed Gleason Archer, p192. See also Carson, p493. Mark 14:62, 1 Thessalonians 4:16-17 and Revelation 1:7 would be good examples. Mark 14:62 is a particularly interesting parallel because its wording is so very similar to Matthew 24:30, and there it certainly seems that the Son of Man is seated first at the right hand of God and then coming to earth on the clouds of heaven; ie, *contra* Tom Wright, His destination is downwards, not upwards as in Daniel 7:13. (This observation is Blomberg's, in *Jesus and the Restoration of Israel*, ed Carey Newman, p33.)

[16] It must be admitted that the end times do not feature explicitly in the disciples' question that triggers the Luke 21 discourse. But the flow of thought there may be that although Jesus' first priority is to teach His disciples to grasp that the prophecies and the 'wars and revolutions' of Luke 21:8-11, and even the destruction of the temple itself, do not mean that the End is 'right away', nevertheless the End is something relevant (v9) that they want to hear about (as we know from Matthew 24:3), and which He therefore proceeds to teach about from verse 25 onwards.

[17] Cf Carson, p493.

[18] One way of dealing with the many problems verses 29-31 pose for this view is to argue, as we noted above, that 'these things' in verse 33 don't include the second coming of verse 30 itself, and so conceivably there is a jump of thought here: a

jump from AD70 in the preceding verses up to verse 26 into a digression about the second coming in verses 27-31, a digression to make clear that they should not listen to the false prophets of verse 26, because when Christ indeed returns it will be very obvious. But as we noted, the big snag with this is surely the 'immediately after the distress of those days' in verse 29 ('in those days', Mark 13:24), which seems to make clear that verse 29 follows directly after the 'distress' of verses 21-22.

[19] Finally, bearing in mind Tom Wright's assertion that the second coming isn't in view even in Matthew 24:36-51, it is worth looking at the parables that immediately follow chapter 24, and noting that the first and third at least are surely not about AD70 but about the second coming as normally understood, along with the 'wedding banquet' of Revelation 19 and the final judgement of the nations. Dale Allison, in *Jesus and the Restoration of Israel,* ed Carey Newman, p135, makes the further point that this discourse resembles Jewish apocalyptic literature, which is usually understood as being about the end times.

[20] C E B Cranfield, *The Gospel According to St Mark,* p402. This is also the conclusion of Riddlebarger, pp187, 190, 198-99 – significantly, because Riddlebarger is a standard-bearer for what I have called the more 'non-literal' approach to prophecy. Hendriksen, from the same viewpoint, argues likewise that the judgement of AD70 is 'a type, a foreshadowing or adumbration' of the events of the End (*Matthew* [Banner of Truth, 1973], p851). From the opposite point of view, the more 'literally minded' scholars would usually be very comfortable with the 'dual fulfilment' approach; Moo, for example, writes that 'Jesus "telescopes" AD 70 and the end of the age in a manner reminiscent of the prophets, who frequently looked at the end of the age through more immediate historical events' (in Archer, p192). And see also G E Ladd, *Presence of the Future* (Eerdmans, 1974), pp322-28: 'It is precisely this tension between

the imminent historical and the indeterminate eschatological which is the genius of the prophetic perspective ... The important point is that these two events ... are in fact one redemptive event in two parts.' He quotes Cranfield on this: 'The foreshortening, by which the Old Testament sees as one divine intervention in the future that which from the viewpoint of the New Testament writers is both past and future, is not only a visual illusion; for the distance brings out an essential unity, which is not so apparent from a position in between the ascension and the Parousia.' Ladd adds, 'The thread which binds the Old Testament books together ... is the sense of participating in redemptive history ... This is where the Gospels leave us anticipating an imminent event and yet unable to date its coming ... Logically this may appear contradictory, but it is a tension with an ethical purpose – to make date-setting impossible and therefore to demand constant readiness.' That is to say, issues of timing did not matter so much to the prophetic mindset: the unity of the kingdom's manifestation did.

[21] This is a point emphasised by proponents of a pre-tribulation rapture as an event separate from the open second coming, so that Christ's return is in two phases. One could imagine people saying to Isaiah about his fifty-third chapter, 'Surely you don't expect the Servant to divide his coming into two phases or appear twice, once to go to the grave for our transgressions, and yet separately and long afterwards to divide the spoils with the strong?'

[22] See, for example, Hendriksen, p846.

[23] Christ chose as part of His incarnation to share our ignorance of how long it would be before His return (Matthew 24:36). Is it irreverent for us to wonder whether it follows from this that He Himself would not be definite about whether there were two sets of events and, if so, at what distance? Being God Incarnate, full of the Holy Spirit, everything He said about this would

have been 100 per cent accurate. But is it possible that His reply to the disciples' questions gave something of a composite answer, which did not differentiate clearly between the two fulfilments? Might that be reflected most in Mark's version?

[24] Cf Darrell Bock in *Jesus and the Restoration of Israel*, ed Carey Newman, p124: 'What the Israelite king represented in microcosm, Jesus represented to a heightened, cosmic, decisive degree. What the judgment of the unfaithful nation represents in a smaller form is what the heightened, decisive judgment of all nations and people will be like. The Jewish story has such patterns in it that permit repetition of the type in a way that links the event to a previous pattern. It can do so and speak as if the event is one, linked by the pattern set up by the correspondence.'

[25] Alec Motyer, *The Prophecy of Isaiah* (Inter-Varsity Press, 1993), p289.

[26] Note how the prefiguring is expressed in the way the phrasing of Daniel 11:31, about Epiphanes, both flows into 11:40ff which is about the End, and also parallels Daniel 9:27; but 9:27 is certainly not about Epiphanes.

[27] Cf David Wenham's argument that 'a version of Jesus' sermon … longer than that preserved in any of the three Synoptics, lies behind the gospel accounts of the discourse of Christ, and that all have excerpted and rearranged that account in various ways' (Blomberg's summary in *The Historical Reliability of the Gospels* [Inter-Varsity Press, 1987], p142).

[28] And alongside this, the 'good news' of God's kingdom (v14) that is already being preached (cf Luke 16:16) is surely that, despite all the evil, this kingdom is breaking in to a very substantial extent now; as, for example, the opening chapters of Mark demonstrate. It's not that there is trouble now, and then will come the 'kingdom' that we should be looking out for. This

is the mistake of much dispensationalism. Note how the kingdom is the theme of Acts in its opening – 'kingdom' 1:6, 'power' 1:8 – and also in its final verse, 28:31; the Jews may have rejected that kingdom by then, but nonetheless it's breaking into our world now! (See also Luke 17:20-21.) There is a far grander, much more complete coming to follow, but the kingdom *is* coming in now; now is the significant time, the time we should pay most attention to. And because it's for us that the 'birth' comes, therefore it's primarily the challenges we will face, not wars or earthquakes in the outside world, that we need to be alerted to (Matthew 24:9-13; cf Luke 21:12).

[29] I simply cannot understand how non-literalist Riddlebarger can read verses 21-23 – which explicitly speak of a specific, limited time – as describing 'the suffering of God's people throughout the interadvental period' from the resurrection through to the second coming (pp201-02).

[30] Hendriksen, p863.

Appendix B

Does Matthew 24:36ff Teach a Rapture Separate From Christ's Open Return In Glory?

This appendix is really an extended footnote to chapter 3. In chapter 3 we explored the debate as to whether Christ takes us His people out to be with Him before the final crisis of human history, or 'tribulation', begins. And we noted that a problem with the 'pre-trib' view – that He does, and so the 'rapture' is a separate event from His open coming in glory – is that there are so few New Testament passages that can be pointed to with confidence as making this distinction; if indeed the two are separate in time.

One really key section that is often seen this way (at least on this side of the Atlantic[1]) is Matthew 24:36-44, particularly verses 40-41:

> 'Two men will be in the field; one will be taken and the other left. Two women will be grinding with a hand mill; one will be taken and the other left.'

These verses can certainly be read (in the light of God's subsequent revelations) as referring to a rapture that 'takes' believers away to safety, just like Noah (v38), before the tribulation. And reading them that way explains the very puzzling shift from verse 33, which clearly encourages Christ's followers living through the events of verses 15-24 to sense the approach of the climax of history, to verse 42 and verse 44, which emphasise that 'that day' will happen when people, believers included, simply aren't expecting it. (Which might also be a very surprising thing to say if they were living through the horrific 'tribulation' times described in Revelation.)

But how much weight can we put on this interpretation?

The first question we face is what time period these verses are referring to; the whole problem of relating the unpredictability of verses 36, 42-44 to the clarity of verses 32-34 changes if the subject all the way through to verse 34 is the events of AD70. (Indeed, Tom Wright asserts that the second coming isn't in view even here in vv36-51.[2]) There are, however, a number of very strong reasons for seeing the verses *preceding* Matthew 24:36 as referring to the end times, which can be found detailed in Appendix A (section on Option two). Equally significant is the context provided by the parables that immediately *follow* chapter 24; because the first and third at least are surely not about AD70 but about the second coming as normally understood, along with the 'wedding banquet' of Revelation 19, and the final judgement, not of Israel, but of 'all the nations'(25:32).

A further argument against an AD70 fulfilment arises if we look carefully at the parallel teaching in Luke 17:26-35, apparently given on a different occasion but using very similar words. (Compare Luke 17:26-29 and 34-35 to Matthew 24:37-41.) This will be the time, Luke says, when the Son of Man 'lights up the sky from one end to the other': surely the end times? And reading it that way also creates a continuity of theme through to Luke 18:8: 'When the Son of Man comes, will he find faith on the earth?', which surely is about the second coming. We should note, too, that this entire section of Luke, 17:11 to 19:28, culminates with a story about how the kingdom of God will 'appear'. Unlike AD70 – surely? – it involves its King being fairly visible, judging (in a way that they recognise and interact with!) how His followers have served Him, and giving them new assignments to rule over entire cities. All in all, then, these verses sound much more like the end time than AD70: which implies that the same is true of the parallel passages in Matthew 24.

So then comes the main question. It is true that a 'pre-trib' rapture does explain why Matthew 24:33 says that Christ's followers should sense 'these things', the climax of history, coming, and yet the following verses, particularly verses 38 and 42-44, seem to present people living in a more 'normal' life situation, and therefore emphasise repeatedly that the second coming, 'that day', will happen exactly when they aren't expecting it. It's hard to see those verses as referring to exactly the same time as verses 15-22: if such unprecedented distress is taking place, will Jesus' disciples ('you', v44) really have no sense of His impending return?[3] Indeed, the 'normality' of verse 38 does seem rather strange as a description even of unbelievers living through the end-time horrors described in Revelation.

So as we've noted, a simple explanation is that Matthew 24:36-44 are describing the rapture and the time before it, and that these verses are fulfilled before the very obvious 'great distress' of verses 15-22, after which Christ returns openly. The problem then disappears: verses 30-34 refer to Christ's open return in glory and the events that will happen before it, and verses 36-44 to the earlier, unforeseeable 'coming of the Son of Man', the rapture, when one will be taken and the other left (vv40-41); when (just like Noah, v37) God's people are taken out to safety before the judgement comes. In other words, there is a rapture before the tribulation; the unexpected event Jesus speaks of in verses 36-44 is then the 'next big one'.

But might there be other ways of explaining this shift from the unpredictability of 24:36,42-44 to the clarity of verses 32-34 without involving a 'pre-trib' rapture?

One solution would be if 24:36 refers only to the situation right then: Jesus Himself doesn't know the time of the second coming right then when He is speaking, nor do His disciples, but when the time of verse 33 happens, the disciples will realise it. In that case the people in darkness about it all in verses 38-41 will be the ones who will face judgement: that can be what these verses are about. (Compare 1 Thessalonians 5:1-5, which can perhaps be read as saying that at the time the Thessalonian believers will know that the second coming is at hand, unlike those who are 'in darkness'.) But the big snag with this understanding is that in verse 44 the disciples also are not expecting the second coming even when it happens.

Or, the problem might equally disappear with 'post-tribber' Douglas Moo's suggestion noted in an earlier chapter, that 'Evidence from Qumran indicates that "generation" could be used to indicate the last generation before the end'.[4] Moo proposes that the apparently blatant clash can be resolved in that the uncertainty of verse 36 applies to Jesus' time (effectively, 'No one knows now') and also to every generation except the one that would actually see Him come back; whereas the certainty of verse 33 is that of 'this generation' (v34), who His hearers would easily understand as the last generation, the one that sees the 'fig-tree' signs, and for whom verses 32-34 apply. When *they* see these signs, they will know that, despite the terrible things that are happening, the Lord is 'at the door' and they won't all die before the Lord returns in glory. However: that would have been a strangely misleading message for Jesus to leave for the generation that lived through AD70; surely then, when they saw the abomination in the temple, they would have seen themselves as this special 'last generation', the one that would know they were about to see the End and His imminent return. And isn't that precisely the disastrous error Jesus was seeking to guard them against in verse 6?

'Taken' by the rapture or 'taken' in judgement?

So that might send us back to the 'pre-trib' understanding, that Matthew 24:36ff are about a rapture separate from Christ's open second coming. But there is one more alternative to consider.

To grasp it we need to return to Jesus' parallel teachings in Luke 17:26-35, and the context that passage gives to those key words 'On that night two people will be in one bed; one will be taken and the other left' (17:34-35 = Matthew 24:40-41); because according to verse 30, what Luke is describing is 'the day the Son of Man is *revealed*' (emphasis mine). Now that might seem a rather odd way to speak of the rapture *in distinction from* Christ's open, visible return. (Perhaps one might respond that it is specifically to the 'disciples', who have in the past longed for deliverance that didn't come ['you', v22], that He is now 'revealed' as rescuer. Is that plausible?)

More problematically, however, Luke 17:31 – 'No-one in the field should go back for anything' – is clearly about surviving some catastrophic event, and not about the rapture. (The exact parallel of Luke 17:31 is in fact what Matthew 24:15-18 has to say about escaping assault on Jerusalem.) So, then, a likely interpretation of 'the day the Son of Man is revealed' might indeed be the revelation of Christ active in judgement on Jerusalem; a judgement comparable to the judgements in the days of Noah (Luke 17:27) or of Lot (v29). (In the Old Testament a 'day of the Lord' is often a day of judgement; see, for example, Amos 5:18-20.) In that case, what Jesus has to say about it being unexpected would be a warning to the unbelieving Jews (who in 17:20 were asking what the future holds) that this judgement, when it comes, will be totally unexpected as far as people like themselves are concerned. So then, 'one will be taken and the other left' would seem in Luke to be about being taken by judgement, or being captured ('taken') or butchered by the invader assaulting Jerusalem, and not about any 'pre-trib' rapture. After all, someone who will be 'taken up' in the rapture certainly doesn't need to be told not to go downstairs for their belongings (v31)!

However, when we return to Matthew 24 and apply this interpretation there, we find the matter's still not settled. A reading of these verses, particularly in their Matthew form, as a warning of divine judgement coming through an invader unexpectedly assaulting Judaea (whether that be in AD70 or at the End), and not of the rapture, has at least five problems of its own.

1. It is a little difficult to reconcile with Jesus' emphasis that what He is speaking of will come totally out of the blue. 'They knew nothing ... That is how it will be,' says Matthew 24:39. Is an overwhelming invasion that hard to see coming? It seems a particularly unlikely thing for Jesus to have said if we're thinking of a pre-technological era like AD70 when the invading Roman legions had to march on foot into Palestine. (However, it could make more sense if instead it's about the end time; many will read Daniel 9:27 as warning of an unexpected treachery in the end time, when the satanic dictator will break a disastrous covenant made with him by the Jews, stopping their worship suddenly by invasive military force and desecrating their temple;[5] that could be sudden and speedy.)

2. Even if judgement is in view in Matthew 24:39/Luke 17:30, there is still a case for seeing a vital switch of topic to the rapture in the verses that follow about one being taken and the other left. Moo (not a 'pre-tribber'), suggesting that these last verses may be about the rapture, notes significantly that the word for 'taken' in Matthew 24:40-41 (= Luke 17:34-35) is not in fact the same as that used for 'taken' in judgement in 24:39.[6] A switch of topic from

'taken in judgement' in 24:39 to 'taken to heaven' in 24:40 might seem rather abrupt; but Jesus' vital point could be precisely that the person who has not been 'taken' to heaven in verse 40 does now face being 'taken' by unexpected judgement. France (likewise not a 'pre-tribber'!), notes equally significantly:

> 'Taken' [in Matthew 24:40-41] is the same verb used e.g. in 1:20; 17:1; 18:16; 20:17; it implies to take someone to be with you, and therefore here points to the *salvation* [ie a divine rescue] *rather than the destruction of the one 'taken'* (emphasis mine).[7]

3. Again: when both Matthew 24:39 and Luke 17:27-30 speak about the judgement to come, they state that 'all' the people in view are involved. So doesn't that imply that we're dealing with something different – that is, the rapture – in the following verses, Matthew 24:40-41 and Luke 17:34-35, because there some at least are not 'taken'?

4. Fourthly, the description of these days as a time when the Son of Man 'will be like the lightning, which flashes and lights up the sky from one end to the other' (Luke 17:24), sounds like a coming of Christ marked by something much more visible – to those He comes for, at any rate – than His role as a hidden, secret cause behind the coming to Judaea of evil human invaders.

(Objection: can that phrasing – 'lights up the sky from one end to the other' – really make any sense if it's about a 'secret rapture', where it would have to be saying that Christ's coming will indeed be clear and unmistakable, but only to His disciples? Just possibly, given the urgency of

His warning to them in the preceding verse not to be deceived by any substitute.)

5. Lastly, in Matthew these verses lead straight into 24:42-51, where the 'day your Lord will come' and the lessons Jesus draws from it surely speak primarily of a coming of Christ for His own people; they at least are clearly about the coming of the Son of Man, not the coming of invaders. And, to me most strikingly, is there not a further close continuity of theme between the practical emphasis on the need to be prepared in 24:36-51 ('Therefore' in v42 ties the whole section together), and the same theme of readiness in the story of the ten virgins that follows immediately (25:1-13), which ends by repeating in 25:13 the same firm warning to be ready as in 24:36,42,44? But in that case we must recognise that the story of the ten virgins is contrasting those who are prepared and, because of that, 'taken' with the Bridegroom into the wedding banquet, as against those who are unprepared and therefore left outside. It's clearly about the unexpected coming *of the Bridegroom* (a figure Jesus uses of Himself in eg Matthew 9:15) to take His people *into the banquet*; and not at all about the unexpected coming of judgement, nor of invaders. So that implies that the same is also true of the last parts of Matthew 24; they too are about Christ's unexpected coming.

But it is hard to be certain. As we've seen, there is evidence on both sides. So at least we must conclude that we can't simply assume a reference to the rapture in these key words 'one will be taken and the other left'; that is, we can't be certain that this penultimate section of Matthew 24 is speaking of the rapture.

189

And that does make the scarcity of NT passages clearly distinguishing the rapture from Christ's open appearing in glory a tiny bit surprising; if, that is, the two are indeed separate in time, and the rapture comes first.

Notes

[1] Many American 'pre-trib' writers are also dispensationalists concerned to argue that Matthew 24 is written entirely for Israel rather than for the Church, so they do not see the rapture in these verses. See, for example, Charles Feinberg, *Millennialism*, pp231,298, and Tim LaHaye, *The Rapture*, p204.

[2] Although in his books for the popular market Wright tells Christians reading them as warnings to be ready for the second coming or for their own death, 'You can read the passage in either of these ways, or both. Often the voice of God can be heard in Scripture in ways the original writers hadn't imagined – though you need to retain, as the control, a clear sense of what they did mean,' which in this case, he thinks, is the great crisis of AD70 (*Matthew for Everyone*, pp126-27).

[3] The same question arises regarding Jesus' warning in the end-time section of Luke 21 about being 'weighed down with … the anxieties of life' so that 'that day will close on you *unexpectedly* like a trap' (21:34, emphasis mine). This seems an unlikely thing to say about AD70 when Roman invaders were pouring into Palestine. But equally if it's end time it reads rather oddly after verses 25-26 ('There will be signs in the sun, moon and stars. On the earth, nations will be in anguish and perplexity at the roaring and tossing of the sea. [People] will faint from terror, apprehensive of what is coming on the world'). Unless, that is, Jesus' warning applies to a period before an unforeseeable pre-tribulational rapture; this would be an argument for that.

[4] In *Three Views on the Rapture*, ed Gleason Archer, p253, citing Ellis' New Century commentary on Luke.

[5] Some would see this as linked to the sudden end-time attack on Israel prophesied in Ezekiel 38 and 39, when Israel is 'unsuspecting' (38:11) – and God says this complacency was because of their 'unfaithfulness … when they lived in safety in

their land' (39:26), which might imply an unwise dependence on a protective treaty with a deceitful outside power rather than on God. This could provide a background for Matthew 24:38-39.

[6] In Archer, p196.

[7] R T France, *Matthew,* p348. It is actually quite striking how many commentators who certainly aren't 'pre-tribbers' see something like the rapture in these verses. Kim Riddlebarger (*A Case for Amillennialism*, p205) links Matthew 24:40-41 to verse 31 ('Those who are taken away, presumably believers, are the elect', he says). And in his Tyndale commentary on Luke (Inter-Varsity Press, 1974, pp261-62), Leon Morris sees Luke 17:26ff as a whole as being about end-time judgment and destruction, but in verse 34 '"taken"… evidently means taken to be with Him (cf 1 Thess 4:17)' – that is, the rapture.

Appendix C

Twelve Reasons To Read Revelation

Revelation has an alarming reputation. There are many commentators whose discussions make it sound very daunting. The back covers of their works are full of ominous comments about 'abstruse symbolism', 'bizarre imagery' and the like. The result is to leave many of us feeling that Revelation will be a hard book to tackle.

Yet we cannot believe it was meant to be incomprehensible. Certainly, if God designed the Bible to give us sustenance for seventy years of discipleship, some sections may be operating on 'time-release'; they release their nourishment only in response to an acquaintance deepened over the years. Nevertheless, 2 Timothy 3:16 remains true: '*All* Scripture' (emphasis mine), Revelation included, 'is useful for teaching, rebuking, correcting and training in righteousness.' So as we feed on Revelation we're living out faith in the revealing power of the Spirit – particularly as this is the one book in the Bible that comes specifically with a promise of blessing for those who read it (1:3)! We cannot neglect Revelation, because what we'll receive from it we will not receive anywhere else.

Lord, I trust You. Please help me understand this book, at least a little …

So why should we make the effort?

For at least twelve reasons!

1. Because of what it teaches us about Jesus (chapter 1)

Revelation is not a puzzle or a horoscope. Above all, Revelation, throughout, is the 'revelation of Jesus Christ' (1:1). We learn so much about Jesus from the Gospels as we watch His life, His actions and teaching, and above all His death and resurrection on earth. But we also need to absorb the supernatural vision that Revelation 1:12ff gives us, that makes John fall at His feet 'as though dead' (v17).

We don't need to understand every detail, but we do need to let that dazzling, holy purity soak deep into our imaginations. Those eyes like blazing fire, which we encounter either in surrender or in judgement; those feet burning as He walks the earth, amid His churches; that sword from His mouth that is the piercing Word of God … Here is an overwhelming force of life that leaves the apostle (who leant back so easily against this same Christ's shoulder at the Last Supper) devastated on the ground. Our Christianity is incomplete if we have never understood why.

And then that Christ places His 'right hand on me' (v17; imagine how that would feel) and says, 'Do not be afraid.' He does not waste these words on those who do not need them. And what He adds (v18), we can turn straight into an act of adoration: *Lord, I worship You that You are the First and the Last; thank You that You, pre-eminently, are the Living One; thank You that You, the Living One, astonishingly, became dead; thank You that You are alive for ever and ever, and have the keys of death and Hades ...*

This vision of Christ's glory is what equips John to hear God's Word for his culture. But this is only the beginning. Right through the book, Revelation keeps on showing us more of the glory of Jesus. We see Him revealed in seven different and remarkable ways in the seven letters of chapters 2 and 3; as Lion and yet Lamb in chapter 5; as the one opening the sealed book of history in chapter 6; as the wrathful Lamb at the end of chapter 6; as our Redeemer and our Shepherd in chapter 7; possibly as the mighty angel majestically dominating sea and land (and providing the vital 'little book' that explains everything) in chapter 10, and yet as the vulnerable male child in chapter 12; as the Lamb indeed slain from the creation of the world in chapter 13; as the crowned Son of Man controlling the earth's destiny in chapter 14; as the triumphant Lord of lords and King of kings in chapter 17; as the Bridegroom in chapter 19; as the victorious Word of God, Faithful and True, later in chapter 19; and finally, simply, as Jesus, in chapter 22. Yes, this astonishing book is indeed and above all the 'revelation of Jesus Christ' (1:1); and amid all the puzzling and fascinating symbols we need to keep anchored – and worshipfully responsive! – to that.

2. *Because of what it teaches us about local churches (chapters 2-3)*

Revelation 2 and 3 are a series of letters from the Lord to a range of local churches. They are described clearly and honestly. God, we see over and over again, knows – and values – their actions. Some score highly on faithfulness and discernment of false teachers, but – crucially – they have lost their first love (2:2,4). Others score highly on love, but are disastrously weak on the truth (2:19-20). If we reflect on each letter, we learn how the Lord feels about the condition of these ordinary congregations, and what the consequence of their particular approach is liable to be.

The Ephesian church is a fascinating example, because it receives five messages in the course of the New Testament: Ephesians, 1 and 2 Timothy (Timothy was based in Ephesus), this letter, and Paul's address in Acts 20. And here, as elsewhere in the New Testament,[1] we sense 'second-generationitis' set in; the sclerosis that can happen once the days of pioneering enthusiasm (and pioneering blunders) are over.[2] It seems Ephesus had finally learned the lessons about wrong doctrine that Paul had impressed so tearfully on their elders[3] and on Timothy.[4] We don't know what struggles they had passed through, but finally they had 'tested those who claim to be apostles but are not, and have found them false' (Revelation 2:2). A heritage to be proud of! And the Lord had seen their 'deeds, your hard work and your perseverance ... You have persevered and have endured hardships for my name, and have not grown weary' (vv2,3). And now ... and now, with all that, their witness was on the edge of being terminated (v5).

It is painful to read. For some of us it comes very close to home. We feel we have worked hard, laboured, persevered. And the Lord is not uninterested in these things; over and over again in these chapters He will say, 'I know your deeds' (2:2,19; 3:1,8,15). But somewhere along the line, Ephesus had lost the passion (v4). We recognise it all too clearly: among all our labours in God's service, a tiredness comes that leaves no strength to pray, to love, to worship. And our service grows weary, mechanical; the light is going out. The Lord issues a trumpet-call to face up to the issue ('Remember', v5): we need to recognise the importance of the problem, and seek seriously for the Spirit to rekindle that 'first love' for Jesus.

Collectively, too, 'lampstands' do most certainly get 'removed' (v5). There are all kinds of movements that once burned with the fire of love for Christ but have no spiritual impact now, though tragically the purely human structure carries on regardless.[5] Truth held without the 'first love' can soon extinguish all light; such churches can bring shame rather than glory to the gospel. And the 'removal of the lampstand' can happen to people who have worked so very hard for God's honour (vv2-3).

Father, I thank You for Your Word; please help me, help us in our own congregation, to grasp and work on the lessons of Ephesus. (And those in the letters that follow ...)

But after the seven letters, Revelation changes gear. An astounding and inspiring vision of glory is now in store for us. We need to press on in this book ...

3. Because of what it teaches us about heaven (chapters 4-5)[6]

Revelation 4 and 5 take us to heaven. We need that. As we noted earlier, Paul regards our 'hope' of heaven as a spiritual 'helmet', protecting our thinking (1 Thessalonians 5:8). Peter likewise presents a direct alternative between being dominated by unclean desires and being gripped by this longing for the eternal world of heaven (1 Peter 1:13-14).

This time, we get to see heaven for ourselves. And of course these chapters are strange. They ought to be. Of course they strain our understanding to its limit. That's what we should expect! But where understanding fails, worship and love continue. Read them and let the wonder and the glory sweep past you and into you.

We can leave aside what is (as yet) out of our reach, and worship God now for what is plain. There is a throne at the heart of heaven (4:2); one Lord, who has set His glory in eternity, exalted above the universe. This certainty is one of the many enormously relevant lessons Revelation embodies for us who are called to be 'overcomers'.[7] *I love and praise You, Lord!* That throne is expressed through a rainbow (v3) – and we recall God gave us the rainbow as a sign of His mercy (Genesis 9:12-16). *Thank You that, even in this book of judgement, Your reign is expressed primarily through loving mercy!*

There are created beings there. We don't know much about them, but thank God that He has a place for created individuals right by His throne. And He honours them – He gives them thrones (v4). Again, that says a lot about the reign of heaven, marked as it is by the love that Christ embodied. ('To him who overcomes, I will give the right to *sit with me on my throne'* [emphasis mine], He says to the weakest of the seven churches (3:21). *I worship You, Lord!)*[8] So does the presence of seven lamps before the throne, 'the sevenfold Spirit of God' (v5).[9] Light reveals; God reigns by light and revelation, not by darkness and secrecy. Presumably the lamps of the Spirit reveal the universe to the throne, and the throne to the universe. We recall that in John 16:9-10 likewise the Spirit reveals human sin for what it is, and divine righteousness for what that is. And it is by that same Spirit that we too are involved in the ongoing revelation of that reign (Acts 1:6-8).

There are 'living creatures' here too, utterly preoccupied with the divine holiness, furnished with innumerable eyes to feast endlessly on that glory (vv6-8). 'Living creatures': *life* is what marks them out, and they praise the God who *'lives* for ever and ever' (emphasis mine); life and holiness go together. We've heard that denied; we've heard it said that holiness goes with a life-denying asceticism. Not so. Sin goes with decay; holiness goes with abundant, overwhelming life. *(Again, I glorify You, Lord!)* Even if God had never revealed Himself through the cross, still that endlessly life-giving holiness would be eternally worthy of our praise.

4. Because of what it teaches us about worship (chapters 4-5 again)

Revelation contains a lot about singing and a lot about worship! And obviously a book that is above all the 'revelation of Jesus Christ' will give us many clues regarding how we respond to that revelation. ('I, John, am the one who heard and saw these things. And when I had heard and seen them, I fell down to worship,' we read in the last chapter. He had understood.) Why not go through the many outbursts of praise in the book and use them as fuel for your own worship?

For example, we can reflect on each of the three terms in 1:5, and then turn them into praise: *Thank You, Lord Christ, that You are the faithful witness ... the firstborn from the dead ... the ruler of the kings of the earth!* John too responds in deliberate worship in 1:6 – and then suddenly is swept up into joy in 1:7; sometimes that happens to us also! Or we can turn to chapters 4 and 5, with their threefold base for the adoration of God. First, for who He *is* – His eternal nature, grandeur and holiness (4:8); second, for what He *does* – His glory as our sovereign Creator, Sustainer and Planner (4:10-11; where also we see how the only reasonable response from the 'elders' to the wonderful way God has honoured them is to 'cast their crowns', their most prized possessions, in deliberate adoration, and declare that '*You* are worthy to receive glory!'); and then, third, for what He *has done* – His glory as Redeemer and builder of the global Church, triumphant above all through the cross and because He was slain (5:5-6,9). Three foundations for praise; *Lord, please help me begin to learn to worship You for all that You do and are!*

And look at the symphony of praise in chapter 5. The four living creatures and the twenty-four elders sing their 'new song' to the Lamb (v9) (*our* prayers are at the centre of this, v8). Then comes the second movement (v11): millions upon millions of angels join the chorus of praise in a 'loud voice'. In a third movement, John hears 'every creature in heaven and on earth' join in (v13); leading to the climactic moment (v14) when the living creatures say, 'Amen', and the elders fall down and worship.

Hallelujah! One day we shall see this with our own eyes!

5. *Because of what it tells us about suffering (chapters 5-6)*

In chapters 5 and 6 we read of a sealed book no one can understand. But what seems like a closed book will be shown, as in Job, to have a meaning. Chapter 6 reveals it as the book of human suffering: of imperialism, war, famine, economic injustice, plague, religious persecution, and – perhaps hardest of all – the silence of heaven, in the seventh seal (8:1). John 'wept and wept' (5:4) because no one could open the book and explain it. But it turns out that there is someone who can – the Lamb who was slain! Only He can open the book: for only He has been to the deepest heart of the darkness, and there redeemed us and made us a people for God (5:9-10). *(Lord Jesus, I worship You...)*

Here is yet another 'revelation of Jesus Christ', and one enormously important for us individually to absorb. Only here, only in the crucified Christ who alone really understands, can we find the ultimate response to human suffering – and to our own.

6. Because of what it tells us about judgement and God's sovereignty (chapters 7-11)

Does Revelation teach us the permanent principles hidden but active in every phase of history? Or does it show us a final, climactic period of history, when everything is at last 'revealed' as it truly is (cf 15:4)?

Probably both. Peter says of Old Testament prophecy, 'The prophets, who spoke of the grace that was to come to you, searched intently and with the greatest care, trying to find out the time and circumstances to which the Spirit of Christ in them was pointing' in what He predicted through them (1 Peter 1:10-11). They didn't always understand what, under His inspiration, they had written. And if some parts of Old Testament prophecy were 'closed up and sealed until the time of the end' (Daniel 12:9), it's not surprising if parts of Revelation were equally 'sealed up' to John's contemporary audience, and indeed to the prophet John himself. But the book also embodies clear, permanent principles which the Church in every era urgently needs to feed upon. One vital way to read chapter after chapter of Revelation is to ask how it empowers us to be 'overcomers', even in the most difficult of times. But these central chapters also help us – the Church in every age – to have a better understanding of God's judgements, and also of His sovereignty, of how His authority operates even in the darkest of times.

In Revelation we seem to be given three sequences of seven judgements – seven seals, seven trumpets, seven bowls – not overlapping entirely, but all apparently culminating in a climax of 'earthquake, thunder and hail'

(6:12-17, 11:15-19, 16:17-21), which seems to mark the End.[10] Revelation is a book of judgement (as books of prophecy often are), and it helps us see that ultimately these things happen because of human sin and rebellion.[11] (Both in our disconnection since the Fall from God's loving power for good, and in the fact that there is so much evil [war, famine and economic injustice, for example], that would not occur if our race as a whole were following Christ; and indeed yet more that probably wouldn't occur – natural disasters? – if our race as a whole were praying?).

In Revelation we are brought face to face with tough realities: that human sin and rebellion do result in horrendous consequences; that these are not accidents, but that as one evil after another impacts the human race it is because it 'was given' them (a repeated phrase[12]) to do this. In 'judgement', then, the evils normally restrained by God are briefly let loose (eg 9:1-3,14, and probably 7:1-3), as a consequence of human sin. *(I worship You, Lord; You are Judge, and Your judgements are righteous. And I thank You for Jesus who 'redeemed us from wrath' ...)* But even when evil seems rampant, God remains sovereign.

All this is underlined especially in chapter 10, which for me personally is the most obscure chapter in Revelation; but if we follow the wisdom of focusing on what is clear, and leaving – for now – what is unclear, chapter 10 becomes for us a powerful reminder that, amid all the evil, the Lord is the one ultimately in control.[13] And chapter 11 brings it home to us even more, where although the authority of the two prophets (whoever they are) is validated by signs and amazing supernatural power, the Lord nevertheless allows them to be violently overcome.

And that certainly makes it look as if the satanic Animal has even more power than God; so it can sometimes appear. This is how God's sovereignty (note the clear sense of timing in 'when they have finished their testimony', 11:7) and providence sometimes work; God is silent indeed here (compare 8:1). A challenge here to any of us who wish to be overcomers is, do we still believe in God when He is totally silent?

But that is not the end of the story! 'A breath of life from God entered them ... And they went up to heaven in a cloud' (vv11-12), just like their Master's resurrection and ascension! Their apparent defeat was a mark of conformity with the crucified Christ, not something final. And so it is that God is glorified! (*Thank You, Lord – I need to be reminded of all this!*) Now, indeed, is the very time when God has 'taken [his] great power and [has] begun to reign' (v17), and the elders 'give *thanks* to you' (emphasis mine) – *Amen!* Thanks for the planet's sake as an end is being put to its destruction (v18); thanks because the desperate time of a world under unequalled evil is now over; thanks because at long last the martyred saints (v18 again) have been vindicated (cf 6:10); and indeed, thanks simply because the restoration of God's direct rule is *right* (cf 15:3-4)! *And, Lord, I want to say a really loud (like v15) Amen to all that!*

7. Because of what it tells us about spiritual warfare (chapter 12)

Revelation reveals. Behind the outward human events of war and persecution, we are shown demonic forces at work (9:14-16; 12:17; 13; 16:14). Chapter 12 (possibly sweeping sublimely back to prehistoric times and Satan's fall, and probably taking in the time of the Incarnation [Matthew 2]) presents the 'dragon', the devil, seeking to devour the child who will share the throne of God; then failing and being driven out of heaven *(Hallelujah!)*, to unleash a brief period of unparalleled evil on earth (v12) – the days of the Animal.[14]

There are many fascinating things here which we don't have space to go into. Some verses may not yield their secrets in our first or even fifth reading of Revelation. But we can set them aside for now; what is clear is that whatever the details mean, this chapter teaches us how satanic onslaught is to be resisted by the 'overcomers', the people of God. 'They overcame him by the blood of the Lamb and by the word of their testimony; they did not love their lives so much as to shrink from death' (v11).

This central verse isn't entirely easy. But perhaps we may think of it like this: What does it mean to overcome? The victors here resemble those of 20:4 (and of 11:11), who did not give way and are vindicated triumphantly in the aftermath. (Compare Hebrews 11:35: they 'were tortured and refused to be released, so that they might gain a better resurrection'.) God's glory turns out triumphant even at those times when evil might most surely seem to have conquered the 'saints' (Revelation 11:7-10; 13:7); and this again, surely, is the pattern of the cross.

And so we overcome Satan 'by the blood of the Lamb', which has reconciled us to the all-loving God who will guarantee that anything we experience of 'becoming like him in his death' leads to our becoming like Him in His resurrection.[15] But it also is that cross which guarantees us freedom from all Satan's accusations (12:10; Romans 8:33-34). And therefore it has the dramatic effect that Paul points to in Colossians 2:15: Christ's death has liberated us, once and for all, from all the power of darkness can do.

Then, the 'overcomers' triumphed 'by the word of their testimony' (they 'hold to the testimony of Jesus', v17). We know from Romans 10:9-10 that the benefits of the cross become particularly real for us through our own act of confession of Christ. So perhaps here: does not the deliberate, insistent affirmation of the authority of Christ seem to have a powerful effect in times of fear or temptation or spiritual attack?[16] Is that why the 'loud voice' of 12:10 is all-important: *'Now'* (emphasis mine), the time when Satan's power seems to be running rampant, is in fact the day of the 'power and the kingdom of our God'?[17] And of 'the authority of his Christ', because in the 'blood of the Lamb' plus the 'testimony of Jesus' there is something the very worst of the power of darkness can never overthrow; and this awareness is our saving anchor throughout the toughest of possible times?

And, finally, 'They did not love their lives so much as to shrink from death': and that faith made them unconquerable.[18] Satan was left with little he could do. In its turn this triumphant freedom is obviously grounded in a profound confidence in the heaven that has been the theme of earlier sections of Revelation (and compare Hebrews 10:34); we again encounter the reality that the hope of heaven is our essential 'anchor for the soul, firm and secure' throughout all spiritual warfare (Hebrews 6:19).

*Lord, I worship You that at Calvary You showed Yourself the
Faithful One – and the triumphant overcomer. And Lord, You
are the Almighty. Please help me to grow in my faith in the blood
of the Lamb, my devotion to the testimony of Jesus, and my
liberation from the 'world and its desires' (1 John 2:17)...*

8. Because of what it may teach us about future persecution (chapter 13)

In this chapter God shows us that before Christ finally
intervenes as King there will be a brief period in which
humankind learns the full horrendous consequences of
what it means to live lives independent from Him. This is
one of the things Revelation is about, and we need to take
it seriously. We wanted our independence from God, a
world free from God, and God's been restraining evil and
protecting us from the full consequences of that folly. But,
for a very short time in the final phase of history, He gives
us what we have desired and allows us to learn what
rejecting God's rule really means: to experience the full
terrible consequences of living without God.

Revelation sets them out unflinchingly – a poisoned
world, famine, natural disaster, disease, persecution,
horrific slaughter in global warfare, and here the
totalitarian dictatorship of the domination of the Animal.
Certainly the principle of the antichrist has been at work
throughout the centuries (2 Thessalonians 2:7); but
Revelation 13 also probably presents a final evil figure in
whom one day will be consummated, unrestrained, all that
Satan has been seeking to accomplish in the worst dictators
– the Antiochus Epiphanes, the Neros, the Hitlers and

Stalins – throughout the long spirals of human history. Satan, the 'dragon', embarks upon a climactic assault on 'those who … hold to the testimony of Jesus', and this is how he does it (12:17-13:1). Here at last he brings forth a tyrant (the 'beast', 'the Animal') with total power, who can demand blasphemous worship as the condition for being free to buy or sell at all (13:17),[19] and slaughters all who refuse (13:15). In this time of 'revelation' the choice is clear: on your forehead you carry either the mark of the Animal or the name of the Lamb (13:16-14:1).

Must we 'arm our minds' (and train ourselves and our children) for the possibility of having to live faithfully – true 'radicals' – through such a situation? As we have seen, Christians disagree. But – with the Great Commission now apparently so close to completion – the very uncertainty should make us prepare our hearts. Both in Russia and China, something like it happened in the very recent past. 'I have been greatly stirred by reading Revelation,' wrote the great pioneer missionary C T Studd, founder of WEC:

> The chief lesson I learned is that as Christ died for the world, so also must we, His Body, do the same. The tortures and deaths inflicted on Christians will evidently be of such a nature that no human being could endure them unless he was indwelt by God's Spirit. So the test will be a perfect one and only those come through as victors who can do the impossible, endure the unendurable, being specially enabled and indwelt by the Spirit of God. Thus shall God be perfectly justified in His anger and judgment when He comes to deal with a world which

tortured and killed His Son Who came to save it, and did the same to His Body, the true Church who followed His only Son. Who indeed shall be able to stand? Holy-Ghost-possessed men, women and children and none else![20]

As we've seen in chapter 3, many Christians would disagree with Studd. They remind us that the second coming will occur suddenly, when we least expect it (Matthew 24:44); and since the Revelation persecutions would so clearly herald the End, they argue that the Church as we know it must already have been removed unexpectedly, by the events described in 1 Thessalonians 4:15-18. These, they suggest, may come on us at any moment. Only then, with all true Christian influence and restraint (the preservative 'salt of the earth') removed, will all hell break loose (2 Thessalonians 2:6-8).[21]

It may be so. But Scripture is ambiguous (perhaps because both possibilities are spiritually beneficial for us). At least we need to be forearmed for the possibility that the Nazi annihilation of the Jews will not remain history's ultimate expression of evil, but that there is a worldwide persecution to come which will surpass it in horror, and of which the Church will bear the brunt.

Lord Christ, do not bring us to the time of trial, but deliver us from evil; and if it does fall to us to face persecution, as it has to so many of our sisters and brothers, please give us grace at the time we need it (Hebrews 4:16), and Your strength to be faithful in our utter weakness; so that if the day of evil comes, we may be able to stand our ground, and having done everything, to stand ... (Ephesians 6:13)

9. Because of what it helps us grasp about the holiness of God's judgements (chapters 14-16)

At the very start of this section we are reminded that even when the satanic powers might seem to have achieved control over the entire world (13:7), in fact it is Christ who is sovereign, triumphant over the most monstrous evil. *Praise Christ, Lamb defeats dragon!*

Once again we are brought face to face with God's judgements; and, however we understand what we read here, it is extremely serious. In 6:10 the martyred believers pleaded with God to intervene: now He does. And so one particular aspect that is emphasised for us is that God's utter justice and holiness not only *characterise* His judgements on evil, they *necessitate* His judgements. As with the other sequences of judgement in chapters 6 and 8, we see into heaven before the judgements begin, so as to grasp the spiritual reasons why they come. They are not meaningless, nor irrational; nor, vitally, are they mere brute force. 'You are just in these judgments' (16:5); 'True and just are your judgments' (16:7); 'Just and true are your ways, King of the ages' (15:3). The world is indeed called to 'Fear God and give him glory' (14:7), but this is not merely because of His power: 'You alone are holy. All nations will come and worship before you, *for* your *righteous* acts have been revealed' (15:4, emphasis mine).

The Lamb, in short, is *worthy* to receive power (cf 5:12). (All this is yet another example of how our whole book is rightly called the Revelation.) In keeping with this the angel who enacts the judgement of 14:17 comes 'out of the temple', as do the angels with the seven last judgements, 'dressed in clean, shining linen' (15:6). And it is one of the 'living creatures', those forces of *life* so preoccupied with God's holiness in 4:8, who gives the angels the bowls of judgement; God's holiness points towards His judgement of evil, not away from it.

15:8 is very striking: 'No-one could enter the temple until the seven plagues ... were completed.' 'The time for intercession is passed', says Mounce. 'God in His unapproachable majesty and power has declared that the end has come.'[22] No one can approach the temple until the wrath of God has been fulfilled – and perhaps we remember that at Calvary it was. (Does 'It is done!' [16:17] remind us of Christ's triumphant 'It is finished!' on the cross?) But right to the end (16:21), and in the end decisively and fatally, that cross has been rejected.

And there are certainly no neutrals now (14:9-13) ...

10. Because of what it teaches us about 'civilised' religious and economic structures and systems (17:1–19:10)

Part of Satan's final push concerns the emergence of a vast religious-economic system that Revelation refers to as 'Babylon'. Reggae fans may recognise the use of 'Babylon' to describe Western civilisation. As we read chapters 17 and 18 we may wonder if, one day at least, the reggae musicians will be right. Even today we feel discomfort as, time and again, we see evil coming from the soulless machinery of our godless economic systems in their blindness and heartlessness; knowing no ethics but profit and luxury, destroying the physical environment, defiling

211

the moral environment, grinding down the poor throughout the world. *(Lord, teach me to be perceptively holy, help me know how to be radical ...)* Revelation shows us our discomfort may be justified; the devil can be underneath the system.[23]

If that is so, then history's final battle may not be between the Christian gospel and communism, or the Christian gospel and Islam. The final, most dangerous foe of Christian truth may be what has been termed 'McWorld': the seamless global dominance of our own apostate Western system, denying all gods except money, pleasure, luxury (18:3,7) and power. Or in the terms of Matthew 6:24, the final conflict may be between the two old adversaries, God and Mammon.

At any rate, we see here the emergence of an opposition – two cities, two systems – that shapes the last six chapters of Revelation. On the one hand, we read, 'Come' (17:1) and see the godless system, the 'great city' with its sins 'piled up to heaven', Babylon, the Great Prostitute. On the other hand, 'Come' (21:9) and see the 'Holy City' 'coming down out of heaven', New Jerusalem, the Bride. We may even wonder if this is the climax of something going on right through the Bible; maybe as far back as Genesis 11 and 12 – the long alternative between the powers of Babel/Babylon (the city built on human pride, 'reaching to the heavens' by brute human strength, see Genesis 11:4), and God's people on their faith-full way to His promised heavenly 'city that is to come' (Genesis 12:1-2; Hebrews 11:8-10,13-16; Hebrews 13:14; Galatians 4:26; Colossians 3:1-3).[24] *(Please help me get my loyalty right, Father; please help me see which system I am spending my life for!)* There may be horizons beyond horizons here …

11. Because of what it teaches us about the second coming and final judgement (19:11-20:15)

There will be an End. We need to grasp this. One day the Lamb, the King, will be revealed for every eye to see. One day the long, ruinous experiment of rebellious human independence will be put to a merciful end. God Himself will say, 'Enough.' 'The Lord himself will come down from heaven' (1 Thessalonians 4:16) – to judge the dead, to vindicate and reward His people, to destroy those who destroy the earth (Revelation 11:18).

And as we've seen in chapter 5, many Christians see Revelation 20 as depicting a time directly after Christ's overthrow of the Animal at the second coming (19:11-21), when for 1,000 years this world is freed from Satan's works and becomes what it was made for: a paradise where the wolf lies down with the lamb, and the earth is full of the knowledge of the Lord as the waters cover the sea (cf Isaiah 11). (All heaven breaks loose!) Others interpret the chapter differently, as a picture of the Church's reign since Christ's victory at Calvary. Either possibility offers us tremendous encouragement. *Triumphant Jesus, I worship You!*

What is not in dispute is the reality of ultimate judgement at the chapter's close. We have a free choice; the gospel will be presented to us again as a climax as Revelation draws to a close (21:6-8; 22:17). But here, now, is the stark alternative: heaven or hell. 'If anyone's name was not found written in the book of life, he was thrown into the lake of fire' (20:15).

That, above all, we need to remember. *Lord, it's a fact my mind flees from. But I do believe Your Word. And this is what You died for. May it shape how I relate to everyone around me ...*

12. Because of what it tells us about the Church and about eternity (chapters 21-22)

Revelation finishes with God's glorious new community, the New Jerusalem, finally revealed as She truly is: coming down out of heaven, 'the Holy City ... the bride, the wife of the Lamb' (21:2,9). And we know what, or who, that Bride is: it is *us*! *(Thank You, Lord!)* The promise hinted at by Paul in Ephesians 5:25-32 and 2 Corinthians 11:2 – that mysterious glory underlying his whole understanding of human marriage and sex – is now amply fulfilled. This is what history was for: this is what it was all about – the raising up, purifying and glorifying of the Church, to be, throughout the long years of eternity, the constant companion, beloved and lover, of the Lamb. The Bride 'shone with the glory of God' (21:11): sanctification is complete, Christlikeness and 'conformity to His likeness' are now, at last, a dazzling reality (cf Romans 8:28-30; 2 Thessalonians 1:10, 2:14). This is what was foreshadowed, sometimes encouragingly, often so brokenly, in the community of our local churches, chapels and tin tabernacles. Now, in Revelation, ultimate reality is revealed.

So the Bible's story comes to magnificent completion. We watch the return at last to Eden, to the tree of life (22:2); not now just with one couple, but an entire city. This time there will never be a 'curse' (22:3). No more death, no more mourning, no more crying, no more pain (21:4); instead, the healing of the nations (22:2), and the servants of the Lamb seeing His face, and reigning for ever and ever (22:4-5). *Hallelujah!* And the song of the great multitude ('like the roar of rushing waters and like loud peals of thunder', 19:6), celebrating the triumph of the Lamb and His Bride, will be *our* song; because *we* shall be there!

> The Spirit and the Bride say, 'Come!' And let him who hears say, 'Come!' Whoever is thirsty, let him come ... let him take of the free gift of the water of life.
> *Revelation 22:17*

It's all there. Read it! It isn't too bizarre or too obscure. We need it![25]

Notes

[1] Most obviously 2 Timothy (eg 1:13-15), 2 Peter and 1 John; but we can also usefully read Hebrews in this light.

[2] Phrasing it that way raises the practical question whether the pioneering days should ever be over. It is in most respects better to be in a pioneering 'Joshua situation' than a settled 'Judges situation'; the 'second generation' is a hard place to be, if sometimes unavoidable. Perhaps the solution is always to find a way back as close to the pioneering frontier as possible.

[3] See Acts 20:28-31.

[4] 2 Timothy 1:13-14; 4:1-5.

[5] Compare Matthew 5:13: 'You are the salt of the earth. But if the salt loses its saltiness, how can it be made salty again? It is no longer good for anything, except to be thrown out and trampled by men.'

[6] I want to express my particular gratitude to John Lennox for numerous insights into this section – and many others besides.

[7] Roger Forster suggests that a major purpose of this entire book is to help us understand (and this is relevant to every era) what it means to be 'overcomers'. Certainly this is an emphasis at the start of the book, climaxing each of the seven letters in chapters 2-3; and at its close in 21:7. 'He who stands firm to the end will be saved' (Matthew 24:13, cf Revelation 2:26) – because 'standing firm' demonstrates that we are 'born of God' and have within us that true faith by which we are saved, as John himself says elsewhere: 'This is the victory that has overcome the world, even our faith. Who is it that overcomes the world? Only he who believes that Jesus is the Son of God' (1 John 5:4-5). The fuel for 'overcoming' right here is that 'On the plane of history the church appears unable to resist the might of hostile worldly powers, but the course of history is not determined by

political power but by God enthroned and active ... The great throne-room vision ... serves to remind believers living in the shadow of impending persecution that an omnipotent and omniscient God is still in control' (Robert Mounce, commentary on Revelation in the *New International Commentary on the New Testament* series, p131.)

[8] This passage also helps us understand that it is because God is the kind of Ruler who genuinely delegates freedom and authority, even to unbelievers, that suffering and persecution happen.

[9] I choose this translation (from NIV margin) over 'the seven spirits of God', partly because 1:4-5 seem to present the 'sevenfold Spirit' as part of the Trinity, and partly because of the integral connection between the 'sevenfold Spirit' and the Son in 5:6. We may not understand in what sense God's Spirit might be 'sevenfold', but nor should we necessarily expect to. (However: does Isaiah 11:2 give us some clues?)

[10] Revelation 10:7 states that, when the seventh trumpet is sounded, the 'mystery of God will be accomplished', that is, completed; 15:1 speaks similarly about the bowls. It should be said that some 'pre-trib' writers (eg Tim LaHaye, in *The Rapture*, p59) argue that the whole of Revelation is 'chronological and consecutive'; thus for LaHaye the seals of chapter 6 describe the first twenty-one months of the seven-year tribulation, the trumpet judgements take matters up to halfway through it, and the rest of the book describes the final forty-two months. But surely it is very difficult to see 6:14-16, 10:6-7 or 11:15-18 as describing anything but the absolute End.

[11] John Lennox notes that before each set of judgements (ie in chapters 4–5, 7 and 15) John is given a vision into heaven, to see the spiritual reasons why the judgement comes, and to help us grasp that these judgements are neither arbitrary nor irrational.

[12] 6:2,4 (twice), 8; 7:2; 9:1,3,5; 13:5,7 (twice),14-15; 16:8. Note also the repeated 'Come!' in chapter 6.

[13] Haddon Robinson, *Expository Preaching* (Inter-Varsity Press, 1986), iv, notes that the majestic angelic being who here 'stands with mighty authority upon land and sea alike ... finds its message in the unimpressiveness of a little book ... Thus, when the weak, human voice of preaching gives expression to the message of the opened book, the actual speaker is he whose voice is as a lion and who commands all the forces of creation.' This is what happens when we preach Revelation!

[14] We can and should read these sections as having application throughout history. But as we said earlier, it also seems that Scripture is focusing our attention on a final and very specific 'short time' of crisis (cf 12:12), described frequently in the three equivalent phrases of 1,260 days, forty-two months, or three-and-a-half times (years) – when for a brief period God allows humanity to experience the full consequences of its rebellion. Attention is drawn to its brevity: mercifully 'those days will be shortened' because of their unequalled horror: 'If those days had not been cut short, no-one would survive' (Matthew 24:21-22). There seems a repeated prioritisation of this brief, carefully numbered and terrible period (Revelation 11:2,3; 12:6,14; 13:5; Daniel 7:25; 9:27; 12:7,11); it is the consummate time of 'revelation' climaxing human history, when all things are revealed as they really are – and also Satan's ultimate challenge to God and His people.

[15] Cf Philippians 3:10-11. This is also the pattern of John 12:24-26.

[16] Many evangelists would affirm that the public proclamation of Christ (in street proclamation, Jesus marches, etc) not only serves as evangelism but shifts the supernatural atmosphere that affects the fruitfulness of our evangelism. But also when we sense the presence of evil personally, does not affirming

aloud Christ's lordship somehow change the situation?

[17] It is possible that the specific 'testimony of Jesus' here is of His lordship over all earthly powers, in view of the demands of the satanic dictator in chapter 13. Paul (in a context [1 Timothy 6:13-15] where he points to God as the 'blessed and only Ruler, the King of kings') speaks of 'Christ Jesus, who while testifying before Pontius Pilate made the good confession'; which is (it seems), 'You would have no power over me if it were not given to you from above' (John 19:11).

[18] Cf Roger Forster and Paul Marston, *God's Strategy in Human History* (Highland, 1989 edition), p77, on the 'methods by which God works': 'The suffering and atoning death of Christ, and the suffering and death of the martyrs, will finally be too much for the forces of evil ... The church is moving toward the "evil day" in the battle of the Lord. In this day we must withstand, and having done all must stand ... Through this will come the final overthrow and exhaustion of Satan and his power, in which the knowledge of God will fill the universe as the waters cover the sea.'

[19] As we suggested earlier, the technology of an increasingly cashless, credit-card society could make this all very easy to begin with. The authorities would be very sorry: your credit line is currently cut off, your grocery and electricity and medical bills are not being paid and obviously you cannot run up further expenditures. Eventually, since you cannot pay your local property taxes, you lose your house. Life could become increasingly impossible for whole families, yet very cleanly and with no unpleasant violence or brutality. At least, that is how it might start.

[20] C T Studd, *Fool and Fanatic?*, ed Jean Walker (WEC, 1980), p57.

[21] It should be said that there is a further group of interpreters

who read these passages almost exclusively in terms of the underlying principles throughout history. To this reader, this approach is right in what it affirms but inadequate in what it denies. An example might be Michael Wilcock's presentation of chapter 13 in *The Message of Revelation* (Inter-Varsity Press, 1975), pp123-26, where there seems a yawning gulf between the brutal tone of verses 14-17 and Wilcock's exposition in terms of Christians 'reserving the right to criticise' the government in a liberal democracy. Whatever school of prophetic interpretation one belongs to, a denial that these passages also refer to a time of unparalleled crisis at the climax of history seems to neglect the whole flavour of the text.

[22] Robert Mounce, commentary on Revelation in the *New International Commentary on the New Testament* series, p290.

[23] In that case we need to look out prayerfully, in various areas of our lives (our jobs; our media consumption; our investment), for the point where 18:4 may become relevant to us: 'Come out of her ... so that you will not share in her sins.' This is not an easy issue, because sometimes we are called to be Christ's 'salt', resisting satanic dominance and bringing transformation into some very difficult places. But there can come a stage where involvement in a system is impossible without sin; it is (or should be) impossible to be a Christian mafioso, for example. And then we have to 'come out'.

[24] If this is correct, it sheds an interesting light on the Old Testament, where at least five books – 2 Chronicles, Isaiah, Jeremiah, Lamentations and Ezekiel – can be viewed as helping us understand the astonishing occurrence when the holy city of Jerusalem is apparently overthrown by Babylon. And Daniel, of course, teaches us how to live in Babylon, and to experience that ultimately God is sovereign even there.

[25] An earlier version of this appendix appeared as one of the Bible expositions in Pete Lowman, *Gateways to God*.